PENGUIN BOOKS

TWO PLAYS

CHANDRASEKHAR KAMBAR is an award-winning playwright who was born in 1937 in Ghodgeri, north Karnataka. Kambar also writes poetry, fiction and literary and cultural criticism in Kannada. He is the recipient of the Jnanpith Award and the Padma Shri. He is currently the president of the Sahitya Akademi, New Delhi.

Kambar's oeuvre of over twenty-five plays comprises many well-known works, including *Jokumaraswamy*, *Siri Sampige* and *Mahamayi*, among others. He also has eleven poetry collections and six novels to his credit. A man of many interests, Kambar is also an illustrious scholar, film-maker and teacher. He has held the posts of vice chancellor, Kannada University (Hampi), and chairman, National School of Drama (New Delhi).

KRISHNA MANAVALLI is a professor in the department of English at Karnatak University, Dharwad. She is a literary critic and translator who works in both English and Kannada. In her long and brilliant academic career in the US and India, Krishna has worked on multiple areas such as contemporary British literature, South Asian writing, postcolonial studies, feminism, cultural studies and translations. Krishna is also a member of the English advisory board of the Sahitya Akademi, and is on many academic and university administrative boards in the state.

Krishna's recent publications include the translation of the renowned Kannada writer Chandrasekhar Kambar's novels *Karimayi* (2017) and *Shivana Dangura* (2017). Krishna has received the 2019 Karnataka Sahitya Academy award for her translation of *Karimayi*.

TWO PLAYS

Chandrasekhar Kambar

Translated by
Krishna Manavalli

PENGUIN BOOKS

An imprint of Penguin Random House

PENGUIN BOOKS

USA | Canada | UK | Ireland | Australia
New Zealand | India | South Africa | China | Singapore

Penguin Books is part of the Penguin Random House group of companies
whose addresses can be found at global.penguinrandomhouse.com

Published by Penguin Random House India Pvt. Ltd
4th Floor, Capital Tower 1, MG Road,
Gurugram 122 002, Haryana, India

First published in Penguin Books by Penguin Random House India 2020

Copyright © Chandrasekhar Kambar 2020
English translation copyright © Krishna Manavalli 2020

10 9 8 7 6 5 4 3 2

ISBN 9780143447788

Typeset in Adobe Caslon Pro by Manipal Technologies Limited, Manipal

Printed at Repro India Limited

For my guru,
Pandit Rajeev Taranathji

CONTENTS

FOREWORD

As someone greatly interested in recent Kannada literary history, I find myself turning frequently to Chandrasekhar Kambar as the measure. Besides, I perceive this idea of the measure in more ways than one: movement in language, in cultural concerns, in certain kinds of awareness (of place, time and the pulse of people's imagination) and so on.

Kambar's writing confronted me at a time when I was strongly involved with a Kannada version of the familiar Eliot/Lawrentian mode of modernism. Its hallmark was a strong concern with the themes of sexuality and fertility. The myth of the fisher king and Tiresias, scholars writing on mythology like Jessie Weston and James Frazer, and many other characters and authors of this Euro-American literary discourse were strong presences in my mind. At this time, I came across Kambar's main concerns, which to my delight, and perhaps convenience, were sexuality and fertility again. His early writings like *Helatini Kela*, *Rishyashringa* and *Jokumaraswamy*, to name three among many, could, in my mind, be referred with ease and profit to some of those Eliot/Lawrentian concerns. Lawrence also came in as the referent to Kambar's quintessential views on sexuality.

Helatini Kela was my introduction to Kambar, a young writer apparently narrating the never-never stories from rural lore in vigorous north Karnataka Kannada language. Yet, in my mind, the life-suppressing barrenness of man and land, the adulterous vitality of *Jokumaraswamy* (which I translated a long time ago) and the worms in the cowdung that are supposed to make rain in *Rishyashringa* all sat next to the fisher king, Tiresias, the hyacinth girl, Cleopatra and Mrs Porter. And here was a busy creator from the small village of Savadatti, disturbing the literary high and mighty of cosmopolitan Bangalore, Dharwad, and the other Karnataka centres of the literary elite!

My sustained interest in Kambar's work, beginning from his early thematic closeness to some of the central concerns of modernism, to his most recent play, *Mahmoud Gawan,* has furthered my curiosity about where he is going. This seems to be creativity as yet inchoate, and not at all easily definable, by our limited theoretical paradigms.

Against this background, I found myself reading *Mahmoud Gawan* very closely. I have watched with fascination Kambar's long journey from an almost exclusive use of sexuality as creative power to his engagement with vastly different concerns like history, colonialism and globalization. He traverses these various parallel levels—from 'dialect' to 'standard' language, from a small village to an industrial age and world, from belief in mythical lore to awareness of happenings in contemporary science, from bullock cart to tractor. Our fascination with him persists more meaningfully because he does not reject the past(s), only blends the present with it, and thereby, creates an enriched and highly personal as well as community awareness.

We find ourselves moved from *Rishyashringa*, the fisher king and Osiris to a series of meetings, not confrontations, in *Mahmoud Gawan*. We move through multiple geocultural spaces like the Middle East and Deccan India, from the wide embrace of Sufi philosophical generosity to the mean constricting political intrigues in the fifteenth-century Bahamani palace, to time-tested emotions, to Allah–Vitthala, to the largeness of myth and inhibiting history—in short, into a pattern of multi-level contrasts. It is in this sense that the selection of these two plays of Kambar, *Rishyashringa* and *Mahmoud Gawan* (in translation), becomes important for any serious reader of the Kambar oeuvre. It also suggests how the mythical and the modern can be borne simultaneously in an enriched perception. Although we perceive Kambar's apparent movement from the sexual to the global, the main source of his creative energy, sexuality, continues in howsoever an altered form, even into an internationalized and global *Mahmoud Gawan* narrative. This certainly is a pointer towards what holds Kambar's work together.

A crucial word about the translation. From *Rishyashringa* to *Mahmoud Gawan*, we come across two kinds of Kannada— the rural and the 'neutral'. The task of the translator here is to be able to create a language which can handle these two extremes of the source language. Krishna Manavalli has, I believe, found the precise medium for her translation. What is my test? Both plays in English read easily and urge the reader seriously forward. This is a triumph of precise selection and intelligent use of a target language. I would recommend this work to anyone who wants to look at the art of translation. To manage apparent exoticism as in *Rishyashringa* is considerable achievement. Meanwhile, to hold together even in translation a play like *Mahmoud Gawan*—where the source language becomes somewhat transparent—is again a feat of creative intelligence. Both plays in translation are fine exemplars of what sharp and creative intelligence can do in the process of translation.

I believe Kambar's creativity in *Rishyashringa* and *Mahmoud Gawan* has been preserved vividly in this translation. And that is no mean achievement.

Rajeev Taranath
Mysore
January 2020

AUTHOR'S NOTE

I grew up in a small village called Ghodgeri in north Karnataka. Those were the times of the British rule in the 1940s. Some British company had established a huge textile mill in the famous Gokak Falls nearby. We had to pass by the mill wherever we went. As children, we were fascinated by the mill and the houses of the British officers who lived there.

I was a witness to how my villagers would be simultaneously attracted to and alarmed by the lifestyle of these White people. It scared us to think that our village too could one day become like the White settlements. Would our people take to this foreign way of life? Such were our fears. Such too were the aspirations of a few among us.

Then there were the marches and military bands. We were awestruck by the grandeur and the resonating foreign music. We slowly began to incorporate this music into our songs and folk theatre. While the entry of the hero was signalled by Indian music, the entry of the rakshasa or demon was announced with military band music!

This foreign rakshasa had opened his own schools and was trying to colonize our minds. His law was already wreaking havoc in our rural places. At the same time, we had also heard of the freedom movement, of Gandhi and Nehru, and the need to push the foreigner out of our land. True, the British left at the end of that decade. But this childhood experience left a deep impression on my mind which remains to this day.

It is this experience that impelled me to write my long poem *Helatini Kela* (Listen, I Will Tell You) in the 1960s. There is the story of the demon/tiger, an outsider, penetrating the village disguised as the village chieftain. There is also the story of the demon's son Balagonda who had had a British education. All these disturbing elements which I brought up in *Helatini Kela* reflect the personal as well as collective anxieties that my village and I had felt.

Folk culture tries to preserve all its experiences through stories. What inspired my poem, and the later play *Rishyashringa*, is this vivid experience which my rural community preserved in its oral tradition through generations. Language has memories and dreams. It relives the past even as it gestures towards the new. This folk idiom which I draw upon enriches my writing. *Helatini Kela* describes the plight of the village being ruled by a usurper.

However, I had this nagging feeling after writing *Helatini Kela* that despite all the acclaim it won among the Kannada literati of the time, it was not complete. This is what impelled me to write *Rishyashringa*. The play is in a sense a continuation of *Helatini Kela*, although it reads as an independent play too. I do not see the play and the poem as different genres. They always coalesce in my creative imagination.

So, *Rishyashringa* became a sequel to *Helatini Kela*. In the play, I brought the demon's son, the English-educated Balagonda, to the centre of the narrative. The sense of failure and desperation Balagonda feels when he comes to know of his origins points to our own predicament in the postcolonial world. However, the play ends with some dreams and hope for a better future.

On the other hand, in my recent play *Mahmoud Gawan*, I chose the historical mode to reflect the contemporary political turmoil in the country. Thomas Mann has said somewhere that today, politics decides man's fate. Besides, while the Western ideas of myth and history are different, in the folk vision, they overlap with each other. My Gawan is as much a historical figure as a man of mythical stature.

Then, there is the myth of the Mahar Vitthala which is still celebrated in Bidar. The story of the great Savalagi sage and the legendary Sufi saint Bande Nawaz meeting and swapping robes to mark their mission of bringing in religious harmony is also a part of north Karnataka history. The swami wore the green and Bande Nawaz donned the saffron that day. Today, there are 360 ashrams of this visionary swamiji all over the country.

Thus, Bidar has always hankered for religious unity. And it is this vision of religious harmony that Gawan comes to see in India. An India where there are multiple castes, 33 million gods, and about twelve calendars—this India has survived for 10,000 years!

Gawan too champions religious harmony and promotes education. He builds a madrasa which attracts scholars from all over the world. However, his political career ends in tragedy owing to the power-crazy and violent politics at the Bahamani court. Still, I wanted to show that there is hope. At the end of the play, the voice from the sky urges people to wait for the day when this dream of harmony comes true.

I am particularly happy that this collection is bringing out these two plays in English translation. While *Rishyashringa* is rooted in the folk and myth world, it also mirrors the crises in the individual and social order brought about by the onslaught of modernity. In contrast, *Mahmoud Gawan*, which is a historical play, incorporates the myth element to question the Eurocentric notion of history. It problematizes what we have been led to believe is 'factual' and 'realistic'. Thus, among other things, this book will give my English and global readers a sense of how history and myth blend in our Indian folk imagination. In addition, it will highlight how the folk culture that I draw upon is aware of, and responds keenly to, the contemporary happenings in the national as well as international context.

Chandrasekhar Kambar
January 2020

TRANSLATOR'S NOTE[*]

Sometime back, I happened to be at a conference on translation organized by a prestigious literary institution in south India. Soon, I began to get restless. Where was all this conversation heading? Shouldn't we be asking some essential questions about the politics of translation? Who gets translated, by whom, when and why from Indian languages into English, and the other way round? Predictably, not much productive discussion followed these queries. This got me thinking again, as it had done countless times before, about how little discussion exists on the politics of translation. I am particularly invested in such questions because of my multiple literary and cultural locations.

As an English professor from India who has studied and taught in US academic circles what is now trendily called 'global literatures', I grew acutely aware of the politics of translation. It was at this time that I also started asking

* Parts of this essay were published in Malashri Lal, ed., 'Of Folk Worlds, Native Modernity, and Myth-making: Chandrasekhar Kambar's "Shivapura" Novels', *Cosmopolitan Spaces: Indian Literature and Counterpoints of Modernity* (New Delhi: Sahitya Akademi, 2017), pp. 168–84.

myself some crucial questions about what constitutes 'Indian' literature and what is Indian writing as seen from outside India. Aren't such notions of what is Indian and what is literary often formed, defined and labelled in intellectual and academic circles in the West? What is also disturbing is how the terms 'global' or 'world' literatures (despite being properly pluralized with that 's') gather together in one fell swoop all those myriad literatures from geo-cultural locations outside Euro-America.

Year after year, I looked around to see what was available in English translation to make my brand new and updated 'global literature' curriculum. Available translated works often run to type. Mostly, it's the same writers from Indian languages. The translations come in two varieties: those ridden with yard-long footnotes and exhaustive glossaries, striving in the true Orientalist mode to provide copious ethnographic information, and those that blithely plunge into street-smart American slang in their zeal to make the text 'familiar' to the target reader of the West. I began to see that this business of translation, or for that matter of global literatures, was following an alarming trend.

I soon had the sad realization that there was a firmly established global literature canon which we systematically disseminate in Western academic and literary circles. South Asian critics and cultural historians frequently write about, reference and enshrine the star writers who are part of it. Of course, to a large extent, this canon consists of nationally and internationally visible writers from India who write in English. Very few writers in Indian languages surface in this canon.

Having worked on south Indian cultural formations for some years now, I often wonder about which Indian writers, specifically which south Indian writers, and even more specifically which south Indian writers who emerge from less privileged caste and class locations, find the global limelight. How frequently are they translated? Even if they do get translated, what is the quality of these translations? These cultural questions make us acutely aware of the importance of paying attention to the rich and plural literatures in 'regional' languages—those that challenge and push us toward a more nuanced understanding of what we think of as Indian literature. It is also imperative to look closely at how the notion of this Indian literature gets projected and disseminated in the global context. My interest in the writing of the well-known Kannada writer and Jnanpith award winner Chandrasekhar Kambar has been an ongoing part of this work on region and locality. I look at my Kambar translations through these criss-crossing regional, national and international discourses.

Rajeev Taranath, the illustrious sarod maestro and important literary critic of the 1970s, points to the centrality of 'place' in Kambar's writing. Taranath argues, 'Kambar writes at a time when a version of western modernism is the presiding tone in Kannada literature,' but what distinguishes his work is this sense of place which is at the heart of his writings.* Besides, Kambar's imagination is moored in a community history which is disseminated, passed on, preserved and sometimes even altered within folk memory. In his world, the timelessness of myth coalesces with the immediacy of the present. Thus, unlike many of his peers (who imbibed European modernism particularly via the writings of Lawrence, Eliot and Sartre), Kambar moves away from the patent modernist themes of solipsistic self-quest and angst. Instead, he plunges headlong into the rich plurality and plenitude of the folk tradition.

---

* Rajeev Taranath, trans., *Jokumaraswami: A Play in Nine Scenes* (Seagull, 1989), p. viii.

Sometime back, describing his struggles with the *navya* brand of modernism, Kambar narrated with wry humour how the writers of his generation would go off on a spin into tortured quests of 'identity'. He added: 'I looked at my contemporaries and thought, "I too must find out what this identity business is all about." But in the end, I told the story of my village.'

Therefore, the question before us is, how does Kambar's writing, which is rooted in a folk place and set in the myth time—in short, located in his microcosmic Shivapura—translate into cosmopolitan and global English contexts? The answer lies in the fact that his folk vision, even as it springs from the rural, local north Karnataka ethos, is profoundly responsive to his times.

Take the case of *Rishyashringa* (1970). This early play exists in a continuum with his long poem *Helatini Kela* (Listen, I'll Tell You) which was written in the 1960s. Both these works are strongly connected with the north Karnataka mythologies which Kambar has inherited. They tell the story of the foreign demon, or tiger, who kills the chieftain Gowda of Shivapura village and marries his wife. Soon, the Gowda, or the tiger in the guise of the Gowda, has a son called Balagonda. The boy is sent to the city of Belagavi for education. When Shivapura is struck by a terrible famine, the oracle prophesies that if the chieftain's son walks into the village it will rain. Terrible events follow. We are taken into the mystery at the heart of this story.

Kambar plays with the powerful local as well as pan-Indian myth of Rishyashringa, the pure and celibate boy-sage who can bring rain. At the same time, he also pulls into the whorl of this troubling narrative some of the major concerns of his times, like the loss of self, the question of legitimacy and the sterility of land and human life. However, in the final analysis, the solution to man's predicament which the play offers is not individual redemption. The Shivapura community must recognize the foreigner who is already within the self. He must be destroyed. Only then can it rain and Shivapura survive.

Talking about this play, Kambar has often alluded to how, even in his childhood, his village was acutely aware of the presence of the British in India. The colonial domination brought about cultural crises and the loss of the mythologies of indigenous communities. It is also this historical sense that impels Kambar to rework the original Rishyashringa myth. Among other things, this play challenges a translator greatly because of the rich north Karnataka idiom that Kambar uses.

On the other hand, in his latest play, *Mahmoud Gawan*, Kambar turns to the historical genre. The play brings to the reader a slice of fifteenth-century Bahamani history in north Karnataka. The eponymous high-minded protagonist, Gawan, comes to India from Iran because he is inspired by the legendary fourteenth-century Sufi saint Bande Nawaz. But the political intrigues and power struggles in the Bahamani court on the one hand and the divisive forces of religion, nationality, caste and class on the other result in his tragic death.

As Gawan awaits his execution, the god Vitthala walks into the Bahamani court as a Dalit Mahar messenger. He brings a bag of gold as payment for grain from the royal granary that the kind Gawan had distributed to his famine-struck village. In this play, Allah and Vitthala fuse together.

Kambar says that he chose to write about this particular moment in Indian history because it reflects the contemporary turmoil in the country. Interestingly, in this play, he moves somewhat away from north Karnataka folk language. Instead, he chooses a more cosmopolitan and urban Kannada style. While this lends more easily to translation into English, the challenge here is of a different kind. In this cross-genre experiment, Kambar turns the historical genre on its head. History blends seamlessly with myth. The challenge is of keeping close to the controlled manner of storytelling that Kambar adopts, even as he invests the narrative with strong emotional content.

In both *Rishyashringa* and *Mahmoud Gawan*, Kambar responds to the political, cultural and literary ferment of his times. He raises the issues of history, modernity and the global imaginary in a crucial manner. It is this rooted as well as global dimension of his writing that I have tried to capture in my translations. However, the challenges of translating Kambar's works confront you at plural levels. The north Karnataka rural language that Kambar employs is steeped in the mythical imagination of a folk community. In my translation, I seek to bring in a seamlessness, a fluidity, between the English and the Kannada texts. It is this precarious but exhilarating tightrope walk, where you strive to preserve the experience of the original but make it accessible to the English reader, that I try to perform. Otherwise, as Dr Taranath cautions elsewhere, there is the danger of the translator falling into 'glib exoticism'.

Besides, I believe that in order to be able to translate any writer at all you must soak yourself in his oeuvre. The only metaphor I can think of is from music. You listen to a raga perhaps over a lifetime, you sing or play it over and over again until that raga becomes your own. Only then can you perform it correctly and also creatively. It is this kind of an intimacy with the corpus of Kambar's writings which I have developed over time. I think it helps to capture the subtle nuances of his idiom.

Have I succeeded in all this? Here's something from the horse's mouth. When I asked Kambar in one of my interviews what he thought of my translations, he replied: 'I always look for the rhythms of a language. I can catch the English rhythms. I have found this ability to re-create the rhythm of the folk Kannada I use in my friend Rajeev Taranath and you. When I read your translation, I feel this sense of "being at home".'

Krishna Manavalli
January 2020

TWO
PLAYS

THE BRINGER OF RAIN: RISHYASHRINGA

CHARACTERS

Sutradhara (stage manager)
Chorus
Kamali
Eripya
Gurya
Yamanya
Gadigya
Doddabasya
Someone
Old Gowda/village chieftain
Seepya

Servant
Yakshi
Deity 1
Deity 2
Deity 3
Gowdti (Gowda's wife)
Pari
Elya
Old man
Balagonda

GANAPA SONG

Ho, we all salute your feet
Benaka, give us joy!
True God, Ghodgeri Gajaninga,
Savalagi Shivalinga, we salute
Sangamaswami of Bhusanoorumatha
And our parents who gave us birth.

We fold our hands, think of your holy feet
And hope words will flow! All of us,
We salute you all who're here
Let all the hurdles in our way disappear!

Act I*

SUTRADHARA: Brothers seated and brothers standing there!
We're just raw youth, who came here
And right away got on to the stage.
The one who wrote our play is no seasoned
    poet,
The ones who act are ignorant lads
If they slip up or go wrong,
Please don't clap and laugh
And don't try that gleeful double-whistle!
No, don't even ask what kind of play this is!
If you don't get it, don't drag your chairs and
    yawn

---

* I have often seen a tendency to footnote obsessively in some of the translators from non-English cultures. I am worried that this tendency makes the translator turn into some kind of an ethnographer. Besides, providing exhaustive notes or copious cultural information also interferes with the readability of the translated text. Therefore, as far as possible, I suggest, or provide brief information about the culture-specific details intext (as a part of the sentence, or sometimes in parenthesis) and keep the end notes to an absolute minimum. Besides, I believe that readers who seek further cultural information will engage actively with searching for it and thus also participate in making meaning(s) of the text.

We make no claims to poetic finesse,
But with love, we give you our little message.
Just think that this play was born here
    amidst us.
Bear with us for a bit, forgive the flaws.
And you, our elders here, we salute you again!

(*He breaks a coconut in a ritual manner and throws the
bits on both sides of the stage. By now, it is getting dark.
Village entrance. On the right of the stage, you see a raised
platform. Backstage, you see a crowd. The people in the
crowd are not interested in the Prelude taking place on
the fore-stage. With a vacant look in their eyes, they move
slowly and gather around the platform once the Prelude is
over. In the Prelude, the acting, dialogue and the manner
should all follow the style of the traditional folk play*
Srikrishnaparijatha)[1]

SUTRADHARA: How can I tell you of this? And how can I not?
               Whatever I say, our words will sound
               Like the clatter of broken pots and pans,
               You miss the inner voice here, I know.
               We say something, it means another thing—
               True, there's no rhyme or reason! But we can't
                   walk away from this
               We try to grasp 'it' in our words, grasp it and
                   see!
               We struggle hard, yet when we open our lips
               We are saying something, and you are hearing
                   another thing.
               Of course, you make sense of nothing!
               Where did we start, and where did we end?
               All right, enough of this rant, let's get to
                   business

We'll go on the stage to act, but the play isn't
new
If you ask me, so what? Life's a play too, right?
Our faces are the theatres where this drama
unfolds,
God, what a lot of the daily drama!
Starts in the morning and goes on till you go
to bed
What pretensions, what masks!
Oh, True God, I pray to you,
Make the inside and outside seamless and
one!
But who knows, where, how, and in which
cave He is hiding!
Meanwhile, we talk, drink, eat and walk—
We don't know who we are, do we?
Sometimes, when we bathe in the well—
We seem to recognize ourselves in the water.
And stretch our hands to touch it,
When we try to touch, it slips from our grasp,
When we try to grasp, it slithers from our
hold,
In the end, you just want to pinch your nose
and weep.
But weeping when you see a corpse is such an
old custom!
Anyway, what do we do now?
In the big mortar house, a huge tiger has
got in
There isn't a drop of rain, there's no crop in
the field.
The seeds we planted are burnt, the parched
earth is cracked,

With cracks like so many gaping mouths!
People's faces look burnt, the green fields
    have all gone dry.
We sweat, but the sweat refuses to flow
Out of the leathery bags of our skin
We stand under the open sky, exactly here,
    we stand!
This sky-roof should have leaked like hell by
    now
You and I should have ploughed the soft earth
And planted seeds, but look, Shiva!
The calves born would have turned into bulls
    long ago,
But there was no food, so we ground their
    bones and ate
People started leaving the village then
Still the sky showed no mercy.
Who'll set things right now? Who'll settle
    the accounts?
Not even a small grain of hope, Oh, the great
    Saint Basava, Basava!
We think of all this through the day, and we
    feel
That a man born on this earth should either
    be a butcher
Or just turn into some dumb cattle.

(*The outcaste Kamali enters, comes to the centre stage, gets
scared, and instantly runs inside*)

Oh, even as I was telling you all this, didn't
    some girl fly in
And fly out of the stage? Who's she?
Hey, who, who is she? Appu, Chorus . . .

CHORUS: (*Enters*)

> Why did you call me? Why did you call?
> The moment you see a girl, you open your
>   eyes wide
> And go chasing after her. Okay, where's she?

SUTRADHARA: Wait, don't be such in a hurry. See there?
Let's ask her who she is, go, call her.

CHORUS: (*Doesn't leave. Stands there describing her*)

> What arching eyebrows!
> And her kohl-rimmed eyes,
> Who's she with that slim parting of hair?

SUTRADHARA: She will go away, go call her, man!

CHORUS:

> She who walks fast
> But keeps turning back
> Who's this beauty shooting sidelong glances
>   at us?

SUTRADHARA: She'll go further away, shout, call her, man!

CHORUS:

> With that tiny length of veil,
> Saree draped in small folds
> The girl who's like lightning, who's she now?

SUTRADHARA: Hey, I'm telling you, she'll disappear, call her.

CHORUS:

> Hey, you, Paribya is calling, come here
> Chew some betel nut and leaf with us,
> Come let's chat for a while,
> Hey, come, you . . .

(*Both fall silent for a bit. They keep looking in the direction
in which the girl has gone. Kamali slowly reappears on
the right-hand side of the stage and stands there. She has*

a pot of milk in her left hand. Her posture and clothes are like that of the milk maid in the Parijata play. She shows no interest in the chorus at all)

SUTRADHARA: The sun has sunk into his mother's womb
And at a time like this,
Holding a milk pot and swinging your arms,
You are walking away from us—Sister,
Who're you?

CHORUS: (*Looking at Kamali who is standing still*)
Ah, she stands there like a tall palm tree!
God gave her a face and a mouth too, didn't
He?
Try talking to her again.

SUTRADHARA: Sister, who're you who has come here?

KAMALI: Hey, who're you—
You who pesters young girls to tell him their
names?

CHORUS: People call him the 'meti tala', he who catches
the likes of you,
Those who wander at all odd hours of the day.
He is the sutradhara who directs people
onstage
They call him Paraboo, he who is here, there
and everywhere
And me, they call me the Chorus.

(*He waits for her response. But seeing that she is still silent, says*)

She is unyielding like a damp, swollen straw
bed!

Why? Is she so vain
Because she wears scented oil in her hair?

SUTRADHARA: Sister, who're you who's here?
What is your good name?

CHORUS: Ask her in our language, man! The mothers
and sisters in your alley,
Those that ate the shit-grains, what did they
name you, girl?

KAMALI: Appa, Sutradhara, should I tell you really?

SUTRADHARA: If you do, I'll know your name
These few sitting here, they'll know it too.

CHORUS: And I'll know too.

KAMALI: Sutradhara, neem tree on the right,
Coconut palm on the left, in the middle is
that outcaste neighbourhood
Where I live.
I'm the outcaste Pari's daughter,
They call me Kamali, you see? Kamali?

CHORUS: Pari? Okay, all the calves in this village
Turned into bulls between her thighs, oh
yes!

SUTRADHARA: Avoo, Kamala!
At this hour, when it's already dark
Instead of sitting on the straw bed
In front of your house,
Why have you come into this gathering
holding a pot of milk?
And why, earlier, did you try to leave?

CHORUS: Hey, Appa, don't go on like this
                 She was born to the caste of whores!

KAMALI: Appa, Sutradhara!
                 It's the terrible time of the new moon.
                 For the past three days, I've had nightmares,
                 I saw a seven-headed serpent in my dream
                 So, I want to offer this milk to the Goddess
                      and pray.

SUTRADHARA: Why is the dream of a seven-headed serpent
                      bad?

KAMALI: Ay, Shiva! How do I tell him this?

CHORUS: Hey, whatever! You should tell him this.

KAMALI: Ayya! What do I say?

CHORUS: You must say something, all right?
                 Seems like I was born just to hear you say it!

KAMALI: Appa, Sutradhara!
                 For three nights now, I've been having bad
                      dreams.

SUTRADHARA: Sister, what did you see in your bad dreams?

KAMALI: All right, I'll tell you. Listen then!

SUTRADHARA: I'll listen to it, you tell me now.

KAMALI: (*Enacts her lines, dancing*)
                 Appa, Sutradhara, listen, I dreamt of . . .
                 But how can I tell you of that aching pleasure?
                 I saw a wonder, a white horse with silver
                      thighs
                 And rode him into golden forest flames

Ah, my Shiva, everywhere in the forest had
    bloomed *shirsala* flowers
Wherever I touched, there they were—so
    many clusters of flowers!
A breeze blew too, swishing and caressing
    everything around
He bent his silver thighs, and lo there was a
    cascade of flowers!
The falling flowers melted and turned into a
    crimson lake
Then, I saw the dark seven-headed serpent
    king!
He pushed his head in, and set my body
    aflame
He pressed, smothered and crushed me into
    a jelly
Then he squeezed me hard and slithered
    away.
Sticking this aching pleasure in my heart, he
    went away,
Appa, Sutradhara!

SUTRADHARA: Ah!

KAMALI: Even as I watched, I saw that white horse
    come back
And I rode it, my *seragu* flying in the air[2]
Before I even blinked, there was the
    Nirvanappa hill,
All over the hill, wherever you saw, whatever
    you touched,
Clusters and clusters of bright red flowers!
The breeze blew into every cranny of my
    body,

I cried 'Shiva' and looked around
Saw the golden thigh bend, and a tree
    suddenly sprout
Felt my body shiver, and I thrilled to that
    flower shower
Then the flowers turned into a crimson lake
The lake beckoned me,
I cupped the water in my hands,
But I felt the seven-headed cobra winding
    round my waist,
I screamed 'Mother' and woke up with a start!
My mother said, 'Offer milk to Goddess
    Karevva,'
I'm going to the temple now.

CHORUS: Oh, then the milk pot is not dented yet?

SUTRADHARA: It is not clear to me, this thing, Kamalavva!
Now, I know where and why you're going
The gathering here also knows that
But earlier, why did you come here and leave
    so suddenly?

KAMALI: When I thought of passing through this place
I saw people crowded in here, and I turned
    back,
What do I have to do with people? By the
    way,
Why have they gathered here?

SUTRADHARA: This is where we differ from each other
You at least know why you are going
    somewhere,
When did we ever know where we were
    going?

Like those who have forgotten something,
We kept searching and searching, then, we
    gathered here!
But we can't remember what we've forgotten!
So, what do we really search for?
In the white morning and the evening skies
A dry colour spreads and mocks us.
There's not even a loincloth length of shade!
And all the time, this earth is ready, waiting
    to be ploughed.

CHORUS: Everyone has a problem, yes, but yours is
    something special!
Can't you speak clearly? What does it cost
    you to do that?
My good man, these days people can't even
    understand simple sentences.
And you go speaking in riddles, do you?
Look, Kamalavva, the promised rain hasn't
    come,
We fed the whole village and prayed in wet
    clothes
But the sky hasn't relented
Shouldn't the sky respond? Gowda's son
    Balagonda
Had gone to the city to do his schooling,
He is done now and will be back today.
The day before yesterday, Parembi Karevva
    possessed the priest
She prophesied, 'If the Gowda's son comes
    and walks three steps
To the entrance of the village, it'll rain in
    torrents,'

Why only three? We made a platform
    measuring five steps from that entrance!
Yes, we've done everything. Now, let him step
    in and bring us luck
Let it rain in torrents! We stand here waiting
    at the entrance.
The sun is setting and it's getting dark
He should be here any moment now.

SUTRADHARA: Avoo, Kamalavva,
You're going to worship Karevva anyway
Please go and pray that like the milk you
    shower on the Goddess
Let the sky send forth showers to our village.

KAMALI: Yes, Sutradhara. Shall I leave now?
Appoo, Chorus, shall I leave now?

(*Exit*)

(*The Prelude is over. The sutradhara is addressing the audience as if in a soliloquy. Meanwhile, all those at the back emerge and gather around the platform*)

SUTRADHARA: Waiting, watching, waiting—
We wait because we can do nothing else
We wait until our senses go numb,
So numb that we don't even wake
If someone pinches our little pinkie finger
All right, we'll wait even if our bodies grow
    numb
Only, like an old ache it keeps nagging . . .
Doesn't look like this raft will save us.
It certainly won't save us from drowning
We have no strength to swim back,

We can't, of course, believe in anything
Because there's really no raft at all!
God, if we just realize what we're doing!
The sun is setting, and it's getting dark
Why hasn't he come yet?

ERIPYA:　　Another man dead! Bharimya is gone. I feel
　　　　　so anxious, man!

GURYA:　　This is what happens to such beggars;
　　　　　What of that? Actually, you and I don't
　　　　　matter either.

YAMANYA:　Hey, do tell us what happened.

ERIPYA:　　Look, here comes a good man! Hey, why do
　　　　　you act like you know nothing?

YAMANYA:　Yoy, really! I swear on Nirvanappa and my soul,
　　　　　I don't know. Let all be well!

GADIGYA:　That messenger-caste Bharimya? He died
　　　　　today.

YAMANYA:　Ayooo, I know that too. But how did he go?

ERIPYA:　　In the dead of the night, Old Gowda called
　　　　　Bharimya—
　　　　　He said to him, 'You whoreson, go to the
　　　　　outcaste Yamani's house,
　　　　　Ask her to come to my place early this
　　　　　morning.'
　　　　　So, this whoreson goes and knocks on
　　　　　Yamani's door—
　　　　　And finds it open. He wondered,
　　　　　'Ah, Yamani leaves the door open at this hour!'

He entered, no light, all was dark . . .
Still, he entered waving his arms, reached the
    straw bed there.
Yamani slept on it. 'Probably, she hadn't any
    customers today
So, she has kept the door open,' thought our
    whoreson,
And instantly loosened his *dhotra*!
A moment turned into an hour, and after the
    horny bastard cooled off,
He called out to her. She didn't speak. He
    shook her. She didn't wake up.
Touched her. Her body was freezing cold!
He screamed once and must have realized
    something else too.
Horrified by what he'd done, he lost his mind
And ran out singing loudly, he
Woke up Sita, took a lantern, and went back
    to check
Yamani had really conked off, her eyes wide
    open.
This son of a bitch screamed and also conked
    off right there!

YAMANYA: First of all, how did Yamani die?

GURYA: It seems Pari actually saw the Old Gowda
        enter Yamani's house
        At the twilight hour. Who knows what's true
        and what isn't!

GADIGYA: Overall, I think it is Shiva's mystery!
        We neither saw nor heard anything there
        Why should we gossip, right?

SUTRADHARA: The sun has set and it's dark already. Why
               hasn't he come yet?

GURYA: Didn't he say he'd be here soon?

ERIPYA: He said he'd be here any moment. Boy, why
               aren't you here?

DODDABASYA: (*Enters looking excited. Sits down, wiping off
               his sweat*) Another gone!

ERIPYA: Who else is gone?
               I didn't count all these people here
               No, not me at least! But why did you go there
               to die?

DODDABASYA: Yes, it indeed felt like I was going to die,
               my boy!
               We went to dig a grave for Bharimya.
               Even before we had dug up to our knees—
               right there
               We saw a fresh corpse, hands crossed over the
               chest,
               Sitting cross-legged, eyes closed—yes—just
               Sat there, Appa!

YAMANYA: Hey, yes, yes, man! That's Guriyva of the
               Jangama clan.
               He died just the other day . . .

DODDABASYA: What did we know? Night time,
               Of what use is a tiny lantern?
               We thought we were at an old grave and
               dug it.
               It was like the fresh earth under a neem tree
               New shirt, new dhotra, big turban

We wanted to talk to that fellow!
Meanwhile, you see, the corpse kicked,
    stretched his hand,
Bared his teeth and screamed and screamed!
Shepherd Kurya fell
The rest of us clutched our hearts
And ran for our lives
Shiva, Madeva, and now you all look like that
    corpse to me!

YAMANYA: You survived because you're tough
                Look man, whenever somebody dies, I feel
                    like I'm the one who is dead!

SUTRADHARA: The sun has set and it's dark already. Why
                hasn't he come yet?

GADIGYA: This is what happened the other day;
                I went to my field to check how soft the earth
                    was down below
                I took my spade with me and was about to
                    start digging . . .
                I saw a grave on my left and a grave on my
                    right—
                Then the grave on the left opened, I grew
                    faint
                I couldn't even hear my own screams!
                It felt like someone had dragged me into the
                    grave, rolled me like
                A tobacco leaf and then chewed me up! Then,
                    like a gob of spit, I sprang up,
                Stuck the turban under my arm and ran
                Back home. When I tried to scratch myself,
                I couldn't even lift my hand! My wife asked me,

'Did you go to that outcaste Pari's house?'
From that day onwards, I feel like I have lost
    something,
You know, like I lost something? Why're you
    sitting quiet?
Say something, man!

YAMANYA: Hey, enough for now. Be quiet!
I feel kind of scared.

GURYA: Think that it is morning now,
You won't feel scared.

SUTRADHARA: The sun has set. It's dark already. Why hasn't
    he come yet?

GADIGYA: Until then, you say something.

GURYA: Whatever should I say?

GADIGYA: Something. Anything. Are there any rules
    for that?
If there is a lot of noise around, you don't feel
    so scared.
What, Appa? Speak, speak now.

GURYA: What should I say?

SUTRADHARA: Just something! Didn't we all talk just now,
Like farting underwater?
Say that the bull gave birth
Say that the hill cave spoke
Say *chinni-dandu*, sleep, top, something
Ask, 'How're things, Sangayya?'
Say trrrr, say tsssss—
Handol, bandol

A deer, chikalaka bakalaka
Row of horses, Hanumantaraya
Baby say, say, baby, say,
Strip your loincloth, strip away![3]

(*Backstage, Kamali screams, 'Ayyooo, come, Yappa, save me'*)

SUTRADHARA: Hey, go see what happened, someone is in danger!

CHORUS: That's the outcaste Kamali belching. Don't bother.

(*Backstage, Kamali screams again, 'Ayyooo, come, Yappa, save me'*)

CHORUS: See, she even belches in tune! (*Kamali enters, weeping*)

KAMALI: Come, Yappa, save me!

SUTRADHARA: What happened? What happened?

KAMALI: Everything happened!

CHORUS: (*Pushing the sutradhara aside*) What all happened?

KAMALI: All that shouldn't have happened.

CHORUS: What do you mean by all that shouldn't have happened?

KAMALI: The milk is spilt.

CHORUS: Did some cat come there?

KAMALI: Someone came there.

CHORUS: Who came? What did he look like?

KAMALI: He rode a white horse, and he wore a silk
turban
From under that sleek moustache, he flashed
me a smile
Then he drew the reins in and stopped.
He got off the horse and came up to me . . .

CHORUS: Okay, he came. What did he do after coming
to you?

KAMALI: He held my seragu.

CHORUS: Right, he held it. And then did what?

KAMALI: He held me, and holding, asked me for the milk
Asking this, he snatched my pot . . .
He held, he asked, he snatched
He put his mouth to the pot and drank in gulps,
I felt dizzy—
Before I could blink, he'd mounted the horse
again.

CHORUS: Ah, he must have mounted! After all, what
else is there to do after drinking the milk?

SUTRADHARA: Where was he from? Which village? What
place?

KAMALI: When I asked him his name,
He kissed the chain of pearls around his neck
Flung it at me and flew away on the horse.

SUTRADHARA: Who could that be, Kamalavva?
You take this chain of pearls and go back
home

Today or tomorrow, we'll know who he is.

CHORUS: That's what I say too! When the taste of
                 that milk
                 Still lingers on his tongue,
                 How can he not come back again?
                 He'll come, you go now, poor girl!
                 She looks like she's simply wilting away
                 Couldn't he guess this would happen? You go
                 now, girl.

(*Kamali goes weeping. Backstage, you hear women
singing*)

BACKSTAGE: From a better land than ours, the young Bala
                 has come
                 Bring on the girls of our caste
                 From a great land, the fine prince has come
                 Bring on the pretty girls of the village

CHORUS: Balagonda came! He came! Came . . .

(*All get up in great joy, tying their turbans and dusting
off their bottoms*)

BACKSTAGE: The tender-moustached man, the handsome
                 one,
                 Ah, here he comes in style!
                 Bring on the village wenches
                 Get the pot of scented water
                 And wash his feet well.

(*Balagonda enters from the left of the stage, and Old
Gowda follows him. Instantly, Someone goes to them
and takes Balagonda's right hand joyfully, the Chorus
takes his left hand. They bring him to the platform*

slowly. Somebody else among the people is counting his steps. After every two lines of the poem are recited in the background, Balagonda must take a step and finally reach the platform in this manner)

SOMEONE: Come, Son! We've opened the doors of our hearts,
We've called out to you again and again.

CHORUS: We made festoons of the milky creeper all along the street
And now we ask you to walk before it wilts, my prince!

SOMEONE: We lit seven lamps, one for each step of yours
Come gently, without putting them out, my master!

CHORUS: We made a carpet of trust,
Just for you to sit on.

(Someone folds his hands and salutes Balagonda)

CHORUS: Here's the sickle, here's the pumpkin
You split it the way you want
We came here desperate, we did what we could
Now, we bow and salute you, our prince.

(Balagonda sits. Chorus is walking across the stage in great excitement)

He came, he came! Balagonda came!
He came to make our fields green
He came like a magic sandal breeze
He came to fill our lack again
He came like hope in famine.

(*Ordering people*)

> Hey, you go see how far the earth is soft
> Hey, you go and count how many green leaves
> You can find in the village
> Hey, you go see if the clouds have formed in
> the sky
> And you go see if the absent rain has returned!

(*To give the impression that a huge crowd has gathered, the men on the stage make a hubbub. Then, each of them gets up and leaves. There is sudden silence. When Someone returns on the stage, the chorus asks, 'What? Anything happened?' He brings his hands close to the Chorus' neck as if to strangle him, and says, 'It has come to this!' He glares at Balagonda and leaves. Only the sutradhara, the chorus, Balagonda and Old Gowda remain on stage. The stage looks empty now.*)

BALAGONDA: Everyone left, we remain here like their
              shadows
              What's all this?
              They said green, said 'green leaves', mentioned
              the absent rain
              Now, they leave without even answering us!
              Why? Why's this?

OLD GOWDA: Why? What happened? How can I tell you
              all this?
              They came and they left, that's it!
              If you get so sensitive about trivial things,
              Tell me, what can we do?
              You know, they are like cattle
              They graze where it's green, sleep where
              there's shade

And they only know how to chew the cud.

BALAGONDA: (*Turning to the sutradhara*) You probably know
Why they came and left!

SUTRADHARA: Truth-telling will only bring anger, it's difficult,
Like setting fire to wood.
I know, or I don't. Even if I did,
I couldn't tell you, because you see—
There's always something at the back of
    everything
And there's always something that follows
If we narrated only the middle part, what
    could you really know?
Still, you see . . .

OLD GOWDA: This fellow just doesn't know how to talk or
    make sense
Just poke him a bit, he'll open endless epics
    for us to hear.
If the boys ask him what the tiger looks like
He points to me and says the tiger is like Old
    Gowda!
Have you ever answered correctly, simply,
And briefly to anything anyone asked? Look,
I know what you eat, and I know how you
    fart
Shall I give you the count of the cheroots you
    smoke every day?
You gobbled the bread I threw at you,
So, just hold your tongue and stay quiet
Don't bark at people who fed you
Look at the name on your collar—get out!
Go, go away.

(*He grabs Balagonda's arm and drags him away. Only
the sutradhara and the chorus remain on the stage*)

CHORUS: Didn't I tell you? That it was impossible for
                 it to rain?

SUTRADHARA: You did?

CHORUS: When you all sat clutching your dear lives
                 In your hands and waiting, I thought
                 This isn't Balagonda, even if it is Balagonda,
                 He isn't the Gowda's son, even if he's the
                      Gowda's son,
                 He wasn't born to the Gowda . . .
                 So, it didn't rain of course!

SUTRADHARA: In the big mortar temple, the huge tiger has
                      got in
                 So, how can it rain even if you want it to?

CHORUS: Hey, hey, Paraboo, why do you speak in
                      riddles like this?
                 All the people in the village say you don't
                      know how to speak,
                 I'm the only one who doesn't believe it.
                 So, won't you tell me clearly?
                 You were saying something about before,
                      after,
                 And what happened in the middle?
                 Can you explain what it's all about?
                 Give me the full picture now?
                 I'll shut up and listen.

SUTRADHARA: Look, man, all this happened about four
                      decades ago:
                 A seven-striped tiger came to the village

He ate some seven or eight cattle, our Gowda
    went to hunt him.

The Gowda, who left in the morning, came
    back at night

He came back bearing something on his
    shoulder

And flung it into the dry well outside the
    village,

He had the drummers send a message

That none should peep into that well. From
    that day, nobody

Could quite recognize the real Gowda here.

CHORUS: He killed the tiger and came back, didn't he?

SUTRADHARA: Didn't you hear—we couldn't recognize him.
    Not me, not you,

Not even his older son, Ramagonda!

Because Ramagonda didn't know anything
    about this Gowda's secret

None of us knew it back then!

And when the son wanted to leave the village,

Gowda quickly said, 'Go,' but the Gowdti
    said, 'I'm going into labour,

You fulfil my cravings first.' 'So, what shall I
    get you?' her son asked.

'Get me the tiger's milk.' Ramagonda agreed
    and left.

The tiger, which gave him milk, tried to kill
    him later

But he chased it away. and was returning with
    the milk.

On the way, he met the two female spirits,
    the *jakka jaladis.*

They brought him to the dry well where you
    shouldn't peep
He peeped into that deserted well. Inside,
    there's the Gowda's ghost!

CHORUS: What! What did you say!

SUTRADHARA: But the boy was gutsy. He called out,
    'Who're you?'
'Son, I'm your father, the village Gowda!
    What came to the village
Wasn't really a tiger, he was a demon. He
    killed me.
Now, he has taken my form and come into
    the village
He threw my bones into this forlorn well,
Please save me, my son!' he begged.

CHORUS: What did this fellow say?

SUTRADHARA: He said yes and came back to the village,
But his mother was already in the demon's
    snare.
She took away Ramagonda's skin one month,
Took away his eyes next
Then his nose, ear, tongue and heart—
She took away everything and turned the boy
    into a living corpse!

CHORUS: So who's the one who's here now? The
    demon?

SUTRADHARA: Who else?

CHORUS: Is he the tiger who gave Ramagonda milk
    and then tried to kill him?

SUTRADHARA: What more can I say?

CHORUS: Your father's balls! Shouldn't you say,
'Hey everybody, go sit in your graves?'

SUTRADHARA: So, Balagonda is the Gowdti's offspring.

CHORUS: You hid this monstrous secret within!
How did you manage not to die of it?
I'll ask you one last thing
You answer me and then I'll leave
Doesn't Balagonda know all this?

(*He asks, then plugs his ears with his fingers and runs off the stage*)

Act II

SUTRADHARA: Our roots are torn
The infants are crying
We look up at the sky,
Or dig the barren earth.
We've forgotten our origins and our blood
And simply wander here and there.
The green has receded far, far away—
The soft earth is gone,
Only bats hang here
And vultures fly.
Inside, the king shuts his eyes,
'Open them a bit, now!'
Shall I paint the stripes on his body?
Seven black stripes?
A knot for each stripe
A hole for each knot
And an eye for every hole
Through these holes, can we see any white
clouds in the sky?

(*Night. Balagonda is pacing up and down restlessly. At the corner of the stage, Old Gowda sits disguised, smoking his pipe. We get to know of his presence only when he coughs)*

BALAGONDA: Appa, Sutradhara!

SUTRADHARA: Ha!

BALAGONDA: How heavy is this silence!
               Say something;
               I don't want this silence, this absence.
               Even if I'm quiet for a minute,
               I feel like there's an old bull standing on my
                   heart,
               Sniffing after cow piss,
               But unable even to lift
               His tail to ward off the flies,
               His ears drooping, eyes sunken, and wearing
                   a torn skin;
               He tries and tries to belch, drawing his
                   halting breath.
               When I see this . . .
               Hey, say something! Remind me of all that
                   has happened in the past.
               Say ha, say yes, ask why, and ask what,
               Say anything at all!
               By the way, how old are you?

SUTRADHARA: Three times twenty and ten.

BALAGONDA: At this young age of mine
               What all did I dream of becoming!
               Wearing those rainbow glasses,
               What did I see, what didn't I?
               You open your mouth, there swells a song!

Youth blooms, sheds the veil, and arrives
    wearing a saree
Ah, the scent of a woman!
When she appears, looking like a round pot
    of milk
Music thrills, flows through your thighs, waist,
blood and flesh—I must play a new song, yes,
    I must play!
But when I come here, there's no colour,
No sound—only decay and ruin!
Could anybody call this a village?
Even those whoring in secret
Will be scared of this haunted hovel!
Nobody to shut the doors, nobody to open
    them
Nobody to say yes when you call out to them
It's only fit for spiders to weave their webs,
Or for snakes to burrow into the earth

SUTRADHARA: You shouldn't poke fun at us, okay?
We're already broken people
If we remember the old things
We still feel the fire in our bodies!
But then we come back to the present and . . .
What are you talking about
To us who are ridden with this karma?

BALAGONDA: All right, Prabhu,
There's nobody around
Now, tell me the truth
About my brother's story?

SUTRADHARA: I don't know you—you who asks this.
The people sitting here don't know you.

You ask me your brother's story,
But how can I tell you that?

BALAGONDA: You dandled me on your knees
When I was a little baby.
Now, you ask me my name
Like I'm not even the Gowda's son!
What do I say to this?
The whole village plugs its nose
Like I'm some stinking corpse come into the
    river!
When you see me, you act like you've
    remembered
Something you'd lost and run away crying.
Am I some spectre? A ghost?
Will you be pox-ridden
If my spittle touches you?
When I pass by, you huddle together like
    women
And gossip in those hushed tones.
What's the meaning of all this?
Why was I brought here in a hurry?
Why make me take three steps to the village
    gate?
And why think it should rain in torrents now?
What's the meaning of all this?
Did I promise to bring you rain?
It didn't rain. So, what does that prove?
You forgot my name as easily
As you'd erase the letters scribbled on a slate.
When I am saying so much
Doesn't something tug at your heart, even a
    little?

SUTRADHARA: Boy, what's your name? I don't
               Even know that. What can I tell you
               Of all the precedents and antecedents to this
                   story?

BALAGONDA: Okay then! Go, think of me as the butcher
                   who's going to kill you
               And sell your skin in Belagavi city!
               Think of me as the smallpox epidemic which
               Plants a little grain on your feet
               And multiplies in heaps all over your body!
               Think of me as the fire monster
               Who burns, making a torch of the parembi
                   tree-branch!
               Enough? Or you want more?
               Now tell me, what's the true story?

SUTRADHARA: Are stories ever true?

BALAGONDA: Doesn't the story say that the Gowda had a
                   son called Balagonda?

SUTRADHARA: It's true that the Gowdti had a son of that
               name.

(The old man smoking the pipe starts coughing)

BALAGONDA: You pretend that I'm him and tell me your
               story.

OLD MAN: Brother, why do you want to share
               Our misfortunes now?
               Listen to me, go back to the city,
               Where you went to learn.
               Chase the girls and whistle after them.
               Those who sinned will get its fruit—

You weren't a part of the sinning,
So why should you eat its fruit?
If I were to turn back and ask:
Do you even know what happened before
Or what might happen after in this tale?
What would you answer? Please tell me . . .

BALAGONDA: True, what do I know?
I don't even know where this path
I stand on will take me.
To whose house? To which alley?
I don't even know how many
Kids anybody has in this village.
Forget others,
Not even of our servant at home!
But after I hear the story, nothing momentous,
At least some minor decisions I must take.
I too must say my say,
I too must do what I must do—so, tell me!

OLD MAN: Don't think you can change the story,
By all that you want to say or do, my brother!
All that's done is done, what remains is
Showering ourselves with misery.
All right, we'll take that shower.
But why are you so pig-headed in this matter?
Why do you want to hear
That which will feel like
Molten lead poured into your ear?
That harsh tale doesn't suit you,
Your tender youth, your handsome form
Yours is the age to dream.
Don't go painting your rosy skin
With those festive tiger hues!

You're of tender age, I think of you as my son
And I'm giving this advice to you: go away,
  boy!
Leave this village and go.

BALAGONDA: Okay, Grandpa, I will. But at least tell me
  this story,
So that I can, in return, narrate it to amuse
  my city girls
When they get upset with me.
So, what actually happened here?

OLD MAN: When I see your pig-headedness, I remember
  my son!
Same attitude, same posture, same look . . .
He too was always curious to hear stories!
You see, in those times, whatever I dreamt of
Revolved around him: my son will grow up,
He'll be the master of my house, my land;
He'll plant and harvest in style
A field full of crops, each shoot sprouting
  another eight,
On each sprout four birds sitting, once in the
  morning
And once at night, they'll sing and sing on!
As you sow, so you reap. As you sow, so you
  reap!
. . . Che! A bastard after all!

BALAGONDA: Why? What did he do?

OLD MAN: The village accountant was writing names in
  his ledger.
He asked my son, 'Hey, what's your father's
  name?'

But instead of mine, this son of a bitch goes
And gives his mother's ex-husband's name!
It felt like he'd spat thrice on my face.
Later, I met him in the graveyard
But I still refused to let go—
I demanded, 'Tell me, my son, what's your
      father's name?'

BALAGONDA: What'd he say?

OLD MAN: What do you think?

BALAGONDA: How would I know?

OLD MAN: If you were him, what would you say?

BALAGONDA: Why would I be him?

OLD MAN: You wanted to speak your part, right? Do so.

BALAGONDA: Che che, how can I speak? How can I slip
Into his shoes? How can a man
Be anything other than himself?
Old man, what's your name?

OLD MAN: Whatever! Call me Balya, call me Basya,
Call me whatever you want;
I don't even get angry like I used to.

BALAGONDA: Grandpa, tell me quickly,
What did your son say?

OLD MAN: He broke a twig, broke it into two,
He gave me a piece and held the other,
Then he said, 'You are right, no son
Is born without a father.' He said this and left
What do you say to something like that?

BALAGONDA: Old man, tell me everything in a single
                 breath—
            Gowda, I mean the Elder Gowda . . .
            His story, the whole account of what
                 happened,
            Whatever—what is the truth?

OLD MAN: Why do you rush me like you are out to
                 murder someone?

BALAGONDA: Rush you?
            In another four days—no, four hours;
            Why, in another moment—what would
                 become of me?
            What would I be like—I know nothing.
            I don't even know if there are
            As many hairs on my head as I think there
                 should be.
            So, tell me quickly!

OLD MAN: Do you young people think
            It's your right to get angry
            With just anything at all?
            Or, do you think it's all very funny
            Whatever happened in the past?
            Son, if you are so tough, listen, I'll tell you:
            Look, this happened twenty and five years
                 ago.
            Remember, I already mentioned that
            My bitch had given birth to her first son just
                 then?
            What days were those! It was like holding joy
            On your lap, eating and wandering around.
            The moment you planted—

Field full of crop, heaps in the granary, house
    full of grain!
You know what women were like back then?
    If you shook their waist,
Four or five babies would fall out!
Pari? That outcaste Pari? If she came into the
    village,
Even in broad daylight, you couldn't walk in
    the alleys!
She was more beautiful than her daughter,
    Kamali.
Ah, her eyes, her nose!
Have you seen her?

BALAGONDA: Tell me the story, sir!

OLD MAN: Okay, then, you see,
The seven-striped tiger came.
He ate some seven or eight cows
And our Gowda went to hunt him.
The Gowda went, he went, he went to hunt
We waited for him in the village
The sun set and darkness fell, but we'd no
    news of the Gowda yet.
It was so dark that evening
What darkness! Darkness like slush
Smeared on your face—you have no face,
Nor can I see mine
And should somebody also set up the *guggula*[4]
    smoke just then
Somebody who was walking alongside a
    fresh corpse
That was going to its grave!
We were all tired, lost in a haze . . .

Wherever they were, people slept right there!
I got up early in the morning to see that
God had destroyed our old village
And made a new one here!
Houses, alleys, temple—everything was
          changed
The youngsters I saw yesterday
Were already yawning old men! Shiva,
Madeva, what was happening? Now, look—
You'll listen to me if I tell you the truth, or
Even if I tell you lies . . .
Miracle of miracles! I too felt like yawning.
I yawned, snapped my fingers, lo and
          behold!
Your brother Ramagonda was standing in
          front of me! No eyes or nose,
No ears or tongue, no skin, he stood there,
Laughing! Since then, I've spent
All my years yawning like this.
Here today, in the grave tomorrow;
In the middle you've come and are asking me
          all this,
And so, I've told you.

BALAGONDA: Where is Ramagonda now?

SUTRADHARA: How could you possibly find him? Today in
          our hearts,
Tomorrow in our memory; can't forget him
          even if you try
Can't let go even if you try, he goes deep
          within us,
Piercing our hearts. If you look in the
          mirror,

It's his image that rises there. He touches you
 with a damp hand
And laughs a lilting laugh. But before you
 suck in his laughter
With your own lips, it begins to rust, rot, and
 stink.
We keep laughing that stinking laugh,
Become the mirror, become the shadow,
And in the end, we become, we become . . .

BALAGONDA: What? What?

OLD MAN: Nothing. His story turned into something of
 a poem
Brother, what can I say?

BALAGONDA: Why don't I feel this pain that you have all
 felt in the village?

OLD MAN: How could you feel it? Tell me, what's on my
 forehead?

BALAGONDA: Ash.

OLD MAN: Son, this ash is God's gift to us
Look, we have gone too far with this talk!

BALAGONDA: Don't, old man, stop! Don't throw these
 things at me
All of a sudden
Anyway, why should I agree with you?
I'm not a creeper growing in some pot
Something that'll grow only as much as you
 want.
If I have the strength, I'll grow;
If not, I'll wilt. What'd you think?

OLD MAN: I say the same thing, Brother!
                  We weren't the water in which you grew,
                  We weren't the manure to nourish you,
                  So you don't have your roots here.
                  How can a cuckoo live amongst the crows,
                  you tell me?

SUTRADHARA: The cuckoo was born in the crow's nest,
                  wasn't it?

OLD MAN: Your father's . . . why do you keep rubbing
                  it in?
                  After the cuckoo grows up, will it remain
                  among the crows? What're you saying?

BALAGONDA: True. Hey, you . . . (*Shouts to the servant who is
                  following him at a distance*)

SERVANT: (*Enters*) I'm here, master.

BALAGONDA: Go get my white horse.

SERVANT: Will you go out in this dark night?

BALAGONDA: How else should I go?

SERVANT: If the Gowdti asks, what should I tell her?

BALAGONDA: Tell her he went to look for his roots
                  elsewhere.

SERVANT: If the senior Gowda asks . . .

BALAGONDA: Tell him the junior Gowda died.

SERVANT: If he asks why you went . . .

BALAGONDA: Tell him I left because there was nothing to
                  live for here.

SERVANT: Do people from your parts live only for a
reason?

BALAGONDA: Do what I say. Simply go, fix the saddle,
And get the horse. I'll go where I want to.
Don't say I turned right, don't say I turned
left.
Don't say anything to anybody,
Do you understand? Or should I repeat it all
to you?

SERVANT: I understand, Appa. I understand. (*He laughs*)

OLD MAN: (*Gets up, folds his hands*)
Balagonda, I succeeded in what I came for.
When you tell this story to the girls
Don't forget to tell them about this old man,
please!

BALAGONDA: What should I tell them?

OLD MAN: (*Chuckles*) Something, anything . . . As you
sow, so you reap!
As you sow, so you reap.

(*Exit*)

BALAGONDA: Appa, Sutradhara.

SUTRADHARA: Ah!

BALAGONDA: Will you fulfil my last request?

SUTRADHARA: What? Tell me.

BALAGONDA: If a girl comes looking for me here,
Tell her, 'Your king has left this village, he's
gone.'

SUTRADHARA: Appa, these are bad times. Even girls come
                 looking for
                 Men and go chasing after them! How do I
                 recognize your girl?
                 If you let me know, I shall give her your
                 message.

BALAGONDA: Not quite a flower, not quite a bud
                 If this innocent comes and asks you
                 'Have you seen the hero who drank milk
                 from my pot?'
                 That's how you'll recognize her, see!

SUTRADHARA: Appa, even old women beckon
                 Young sneaking tomcats
                 To come and drink from their milk pots;
                 How can I recognize the milk pot you licked
                 from?

BALAGONDA: 'The sun had set then. And at that time of
                 the night,
                 Someone drank from my milk pot,
                 Which hadn't been dented at all,
                 That someone who threw his chain
                 At the girl with the milk pot
                 Where did he go?'—If she asks you all this,
                 She's the one I want.

SUTRADHARA: Then I shall tell her; you go, and don't
                 worry.

(*When Balagonda is about to leave, the sutradhara
starts singing. Balagonda keeps pacing up and down. He
suddenly remembers something. He sits down, sharpening
his sickle*)

SUTRADHARA: Hey, Brother Shepherd, our true saint!
Keep our sheep from harm.
I salute you, Brother; keep our sheep from
    harm!
Unknown to us, our king sits outside
And the outside has come inside now
We're folk who don't even know
The different stitches on our clothes!
And we've lost our way back home!
Lost, anxious, we wander in ignorance
Senseless like some fools.
Inside, on the throne, the tiger came and sat
But don't run away scared, my hero!
Despite the deluge, you'll survive somehow.
You are the cause and the end, my brave one!
You are in us, and we're in you
What else remains, only false colours!
We folded our hands and asked all and sundry,
'Have you seen our king?'
The radiant white yakshi dazzled
Our eyes with the light from the skyline
But you're the treasure hidden in our eyes
Come, Brother, you who can kill us or who
    can save us,
Come to us now!

(*As the song ends, the servant enters*)

SERVANT: Appa, Balagonda,
Look, here I bring the golden horse.

BALAGONDA: If I say one thing, he does something else.
What do you eat for food, grass?
Which horse did I ask you to bring?

SERVANT: But the white horse was not in the stable . . .

BALAGONDA: Why wasn't it there?

SERVANT: Yes, it surprised me too . . .

BALAGONDA: What's your problem? Tell me at once,
                I will steel myself and listen to what you've
                    got to say.

SERVANT: I'll tell you the whole story, Appa.
                You told me to go there, and so I went.
                I entered the okkaliga alley, passed the
                Brahmin alley, reached your house,
                And opened the door.
                Little earthen lamps were glowing,
                And a row of cattle stood like ghosts in that
                    black,
                New moon night! They watched me
                As if I was a stalk of millet waiting to be
                    grazed.
                Far back, in the haystack, stood the red horse
                No, not the white one!
                Before I could turn, look Appa—
                I'll swear this before you, God—I saw
                    Karevva!
                I swear on myself, on sage Nirvanappa;
                Swear on the Evil One too, it was indeed
                    Karevva!
                She had put her hand on the horse's thigh
                And was caressing it! I kept shivering,
                    sweating;
                My tongue fell dead, I couldn't scream;
                My legs went numb, I couldn't run.
                Forehead full of vermilion; hair full of oil

She'd let her hair down, and it swept to the
    floor!
She wore a black saree, she'd smeared
    cowdung
On her chin, breasts, neck and hands!
'Mother who gave me birth, you're a mother
And I'm your son, save me if what I see is
    true,'
I begged and fell at her feet.
Mother became merciful:
'The horse is for my Balanna, right?'
She asked. I answered, 'Yes, Mother.'
'The white horse is gone, take the golden
one,' she ordered
'Yes, Mother who gave me birth,' I said
And brought this horse here.
See if I have a fever or something . . .

BALAGONDA: Aha, you're a big pundit! Okay, salute me
    and go.
Appa, Sutradhara, I'm leaving now. But I'm
    literally at crossroads!
Show me the way . . .

SUTRADHARA: Look, this way directly leads to the outcaste
    neighbourhood,
Touches Pari's house and goes into the
    village.
This other way passes through the cemetery,
    goes up to the pond.
There it splits into five or six paths, then
    reaches the thicket
And passes beyond the village limits.
You must choose what you want.

BALAGONDA: I'll leave now, salutations to all!

(*Turns to the left of the stage, folds his hands to the sutradhara. He walks a couple of steps and turns back to see the servant still following him. He stops*)

BALAGONDA: What do you want now? Haven't you finished your story yet?

SERVANT: No, wanted to ask you something, Appu.

BALAGONDA: What?

SERVANT: You still haven't recognized me, have you?

BALAGONDA: No.

SERVANT: Ayooo, looks like you don't even remember my name.

BALAGONDA: No.

SERVANT: When you were a child, weren't you the one
                Who wore the tiger's garb in the village festival?

BALAGONDA: (*Bored*) Yes.

SERVANT: During the Panchami festival time, when the river was flooded,
                You and I, we'd chase the pigs to the stream
                And pile stones so they couldn't swim back;
                They had to go out of the village limits, do you remember this?

BALAGONDA: (*Curious*) Tell me more!

SERVANT: We'd go to the Nirvanappa fair together . . .

BALAGONDA: Yes, yes, we'd compete and run,
Trying to climb the three hundred and
eighteen steps!
Eating the holy offering, the prasada
We'd roam all over the hill . . .

SERVANT: Tempting Ningi of the okkaliga caste;
Saying you'd show her the tiger cub,
You lured her to the cave in the hills.
Later, when I came to the place so excited—
I saw Ningi crying loudly . . .

BALAGONDA: You promised you'd never tell a soul
And sent me out of there

SERVANT: Ah, ah . . . what fun those days were!
Life was all lost in fun and play,
We thought the whole world was a small
yard, yes?
Like the river in floods—
The same colour, the same roaring spirit!
Don't you still want to live like that
overflowing river, Sonny?

BALAGONDA: (*Puts his hand on the servant's shoulder affectionately*)
You made me chase you so far, but I got you
now!
Aren't you the servant Lasimya, you son?

SERVANT: Aren't you Gowda's son Balya, you son!

(*Both clap their hands and laugh. They laugh until they
cannot speak. They try to say something to each other, but
end up laughing again*)

SERVANT: When we were playing hide and seek
                 In whose house did you hide that day, Son?

(They laugh again. Balagonda gets up as if to mock someone. He puts his hand inside his shirt, takes it out, smells it, and then holds it under Lasimya's nose)

BALAGONDA: My body smells like the earth. (*Laughs*)

SERVANT: Hey, you went to herd the buffalo
                 And fell into the slush with it, remember?
                     (*Laughs*)

BALAGONDA: (*Slapping his thighs and laughing*)
                 Till this day I feel like I'm sinking into that
                     slush, okay?

SERVANT: Then do you plan to forget all this fun and
                     go away
                 From the village? That too in the middle of
                     the night?
                 Do you have any sense, Son?

BALAGONDA: Maybe you're right, Lasimya.

SERVANT: If it were so easy to uproot yourself and leave,
                 Who would have stayed back in this village,
                     you tell me?
                 This earth speaks so much, just listen . . .
                 A seed that falls to the earth, a tree that
                     sprouts . . .
                 If it has to grow, it should spread its roots
                     deep into the soil.
                 This place won't let go of us so easily.
                 In fact, when I went to bring your horse,
                 The moment I told her you were leaving,

The outcaste Pari became possessed.
'Someone has grabbed tufts of my hair and is
    chopping them away.
Save me!' she started screaming.

BALAGONDA: The outcaste Pari? She was possessed?
What did she say? What did she say?

SERVANT: All the bad gods in this Gokavi land
Come and possess her, Appa!
She told me that the time you want to leave;
Isn't auspicious, so you shouldn't go.

BALAGONDA: Look, Lasimya . . .

SERVANT: You keep going back to the same thing!
Listen, until now, everything that outcaste
    Pari has said
Has always come true, okay?
Didn't you meet an old man just now?

BALAGONDA: Yes.

SERVANT: Look, she sat somewhere there and told me
    all about
What had happened here; was that a lie?
Your enemies will say whatever they want.
How can you believe all that, my boy?
I'll tell you this clearly—I feel like I'm talking
    to a pet parrot—
Just go back home . . .

BALAGONDA: Look, Lasimya, don't press me about this!
All I have in life are those fond childhood
    memories.
Let me cherish them; you go away now.

SERVANT: Then say that you aren't Balya at all and leave.
                  This is the place where your brother rules;
                  I'll go. Even if you were to find great happiness
                  On your way, don't forget the servant!

(He goes without turning back. Slowly, the sutradhara enters and occupies the servant's place. Balagonda doesn't notice him at first. He speaks, as if in a soliloquy)

BALAGONDA: I ask you something, but you all tell me something else . . .

SUTRADHARA: We must find the real roots.

BALAGONDA: This isn't my land, right?
                  Didn't you see that old man? He looked small at first.
                  But he grew and grew, from the earth to the sky.
                  Whatever he said was true, everything he touched took on colour!
                  And me? I became small and smaller,
                  Until, like thin air, I blew in here.
                  See, just know this much . . .
                  Some are born with their purpose already set for them,
                  Others choose their purpose after being born.
                  The latter touch their chest with pride and say,
                  'I chose it, this is my way.'
                  But I don't even have a purpose.
                  Where is that great guru?
                  He who is supposed to be a part of me,
                  Who's within me, he who is in my blood?
                  The one who will lead me to my purpose?

All these people have gathered here
To watch the path I follow,
To probe into the secret of my birth, to judge
 me.
If only I had met my older brother!
He'd have put his arm around my shoulder
And said, 'Hey, my little brother,'
Pointed the way to me and explained
What's what. But now?
All I see is a male owl, a female cat,
Or coughing old men—all the real men with
 their
Two-stringed waistbands must be dead or
 something,
Or they must be lying next to their wives,
 babbling! Bastards!
There's nothing in this village
That's of any use to me. I don't even feel like
Opening my eyes to see anything. All
 conversation
Is reduced to monosyllables.
I have nothing to say, I think!
Even if I said something, it'd be like someone
 else is talking!
Should I laugh? Dance? Sing theatrical
 songs?
Cry holding my nose? Ramu, Ramanna,
 Ramagonda . . .
Where are you? I'll wrench my guts out
And hang them like a garland around your
 neck.
Come, save me from these ghosts thumping
 away

And dancing on the floor of my chest!
Brother . . . Rama . . .!

*(Balagonda lifts his arms up and starts screaming. The
sound of a dance beat from the folk play tradition of
Doddata is faintly heard coming from the stage: 'Tham,
thakadina, thom thakadina, thaam thakadina tha,
thaiyya, thom thakadina tha.' It gets distinct as it becomes
louder. Like a female part from* Doddata, *a spirit, yakshi,
enters, dancing to this rhythm. Once the sound of the
drumbeat ends, she ends her dance in a ritual manner.
Balagonda is surprised to see her. He watches her with
fear and reverence. He bends to salute her when she stops)*

BALAGONDA: Mother, the light of our eyes;
               White Goddess who dazzles us thus—
               Who're you, Mother? Oh, joy-giver!
               Do give me a clue.

YAKSHI: Son, my boy, think of me as someone
               Who worshipped the revered feet of
                    Ramagonda,
               That brave brother you had.
               And I like the way you speak, my lad!

BALAGONDA: Mother who shines like a beacon
               To dispel all my doubts,
               Teach me to know myself
               And save me, Mother
               Oh, joy-giver!

YAKSHI: Your brother has sent you a jewel;
               Spread your seragu to hold it, child.
               It's a gem; wear it on your head—
               And if you sleep with that innocent who
                    carries a pot of milk

Your sweat will pour out like the rain.
In the end, Rama will come and make himself
    seen.
Until then, do what I've asked dutifully, and
    be very careful!
My prayers are with you; I'll leave now, boy.
What you do gives me great joy.

BALAGONDA: (*Receives the gem she gives, presses it reverently
    to his eyes, and salutes her*)
    Yes, Mother, oh joy-giver!

(*Meanwhile, you hear another dance rhythm, 'Laali,
laalima, laalima, laalima', from Doddata. The yakshi
disappears, dancing. Balagonda bears the gem and moves
to the right of the stage. The old man, the old Gowda who
had been hiding until now, moves centre stage. He watches
the direction in which Balagonda has left and makes some
mental calculations. Suddenly, he seems to have found a
solution. He disappears in the opposite direction.*)

Act III

(*Midnight. Three fearful-looking women sit on a platform on the stage. The sutradhara appears on the fore-stage and is watching them.*)

SUTRADHARA: Half the play is over,
But new people are still coming in!
I wanted to leave, making sure that everyone
    is here
But three more have come and sat on the
    stage.
They look like devils, who could they be?
No vermilion on anyone's forehead . . .
They are widows for sure!
They are the colour of coal, but their energy
Seems to radiate and touch me too—
Must be some big shots!
Let me talk to them first . . .
Mothers, who are you who have come here?
And in this dark hour?
Why have you come?
Please let us know.

(*They just sit looking at each other*)

Ayooo, looks like I asked them their
Names at a bad time, che!
Avva, Mothers, you look like important
    people;
If I have erred in asking your names
Please forgive, and swallow your anger,
I ask your names, I salute you,
Bless me, allay my fears, and tell me your
    names.

DEITY I: Who are you who asks our names?
First tell me this, boy,
The way you speak gives me great joy.

SUTRADHARA: Mother, those who know,
Those like you, call me Sutradhara.
Those who don't, call me Meti tala.
Others call me Paraboo, who is always in and
    out—
Call me whatever you want but tell me your
    names.

DEITY I: Sutradhara, should we tell you our names?

SUTRADHARA: If you tell them, I'll know
And these few people gathered here?
They will get to know too.

DEITY I: Then Sutradhara, listen:

(*The poem below must be recited in a conversational style*)

It's Sunday new moon—all darkness!
In the big mortar temple, there's no lamp, no
    light . . .
I became a woman only the other day;

I batted my eyelids and shot a coy smile.
The rich neighbour twirled his moustache,
Put vermilion on my forehead,
And we got married then!
I went as the new daughter-in-law of the
     house;
On the new bed, fragrant and fresh,
My great husband lay next to me. My husband!
I had daggers in my eyes;
I stabbed my husband all over his body.
My nails were like a sickle, a sickle!
With thorn sandals on my feet,
I trampled all over his body.
My frightened husband's life flew
And entered the body of a buffalo.
So, I butchered the buffalo; fresh blood
     flowed
All over, all over the bed, this fresh blood!
I built a dam around the blood,
Stood at the centre and turned into a wick.
Then lit a lamp on my head
And called my paramours—
Called, waving my arms, waving my arms!
A paramour came, put out the light
And whispered sweet nothings into my ear.
'Don't open your eyes,
For I am the whirlwind, the whirlwind.'
After ten full moons and ten new moons,
I opened my eyes and saw—
Not my husband, not my paramour,
But the old ghost on the threshing floor,
Sporting vermilion blood on its forehead,
Sporting vermilion blood.

SUTRADHARA: Mother, your story is exactly
Like our Gowdti's story;
Aren't you Durgavva?

(*She nods her head in assent*)

Mother, now I've got to know your name.

(*He turns to the other deity*)

And you, Mother, tell me your name too,
please.

DEITY 3: Sutradhara, know that I'm
Komarama's mother.

SUTRADHARA: Mother, which Komarama? What's that story?
Please tell me everything.

DEITY 3: A son who ruled the corners of the world
A son who ruled an army.
A son like a man-eating tiger
He climbed upon the throne a day after he
was born
Then he started seizing young maidens
He went to war wearing gold; came back in
the victorious Banni leaves
He found dark neem leaves and wore them
on his hair[5]
He dragged away the girls in his path; he
dragged away the girls on the streets.
He seized all the beauties in the alleys!
A whole crowd gathered upon seeing this
rogue's deeds
They picked up stones—each of them;
They all were about five hundred,

And their hands were about a thousand!
Each held an axe and also a sickle.
They cut my brave boy up, had my child
        butchered.
They held him and cut him up, over and over
        again.
Then they washed their hands and looked in
        the mirror—
It's not he who had died, but only us!
A son who ruled the corners of the world
A son who ruled an army
A son like a man-eating tiger
The mother of this male tiger—
I'm Dittadevi, know this, my son!

SUTRADHARA: God, this is another impossible story!
Avva, that you're Dittadevi, I came to know,
And all the intelligent people sitting here
        also got to know

(*Turns to the second deity*)

And you, Mother, what's your good name?
Please let us all know.

DEITY 2:   I won't enact my story.

SUTRADHARA: Tell me the way you want.

DEITY 2:   I won't sing.

SUTRADHARA: Tell me what you know.

DEITY 2:   Sutradhara!

SUTRADHARA: Mother?

DEITY 2:   What's the day today?

SUTRADHARA: Monday.

DEITY 2: What's the time?

SUTRADHARA: Midnight.

DEITY 2: Get up and look. What do you see?

SUTRADHARA: The Gowda's house.

DEITY 2: What all do you see?

SUTRADHARA: The house is shrouded
In dead silence! Not a sound there . . .
And shining like the Gowdti's eyes,
There are two lamps—one on the porch
Another in the cattle shed.
The Gowda sleeps on a platform outside,
Balagonda sleeps there too.
All the tender sunlight of tomorrow's dawn
Is swimming on Balagonda's lips. On his head,
There's a brilliant light;
He sleeps like a long, wet wick!

DEITY 2: Not a light, Son! The yakshi came
And fondly gave him a gem; not any gem,
    mind you!
If he keeps it on his head
And sleeps with the right woman,
It'll rain like the sweat from his body.

SUTRADHARA: When I hear your words,
I feel happy, like I'm already getting drenched
    in the rain that is to come!
Tell me more, Mother.

DEITY 2: Sutradhara, what else do you see?

SUTRADHARA: Old Gowda has opened his eyes, gotten up,
               He is looking around suspiciously
               He grows as a shadow, falls on Balagonda in
                   the dark,
               Takes his gem and puts it on his own head.
               He goes to the cattle shed . . . in the shed—
               Mother who bore me, you'll believe me if I
                   tell the truth,
               Or even if I tell lies—inside, the Gowdti
                   stands tall,
               Like she occupies the whole shed!
               Vermilion smeared all over her body,
               Hair dripping with oil; she's let her tresses down
               So that they sweep to the floor.
               On one side of the Gowdti is the red horse,
               On the other, the white one;
               Golden thigh on the right and silver on the
                   left—
               The Gowda goes and stands in between
                   them . . . that gem . . .
               He puts it on his eye,
               And suddenly, he turns into the seven-striped
                   tiger!
               Then he turns into a demon, and then—
               He has mounted the Gowdti's thighs . . .
               (*Inside, the Gowdti screams*)

BALAGONDA: (*Screaming*) Who? Who is it? Thief!
                   Who're you?
               (*Silence for a while*)

SUTRADHARA: Now, Old Gowda has mounted the horse
                   and fled.
               The Gowdti's face has turned dark;

She's started caressing the red horse's body!
Now she's smearing horse dung all over
 herself.
Ah, how beautiful the Gowdti is!
She looks like Ellavva of the hills
Like the Goddess has come down to our
 village
After all the festival bustle, smearing
Bhandara on herself; how she moves her
 head![6]
How she shakes her waist! Though she is far
 away,
She smells like the newly ploughed earth.
Those who have seen her, should capture her
 in their eyes . . .
Aha, she started swirling around there!
She plunged her hand into her bosom and
 started dancing,
Started singing . . .

(You hear the sound of the instrument Ellamma's devotees play on the Widow's Full Moon Day festival. The Gowdti sings to this accompaniment. The sutradhara and the three deities disappear. The dancing Gowdti appears and disappears on the stage. You see only her silhouette, her dancing shadow)

GOWDTI: I must dance, bend my body, until my feet tire!
Like a peacock or a calf, turning and turning,
 like a top here.
I open my thighs, let my hair down, and
 plunge my hand
Into the soft depths of my breast, ah mother!
I sweat and smell like a wild date palm,

My skin is like a hot tin foil, my dear!
And look, someone has set off a forest fire!
Every cranny of my body throbs;
And my hair is now in flames
Burning, burning, I stand like a live lamp
　　　post!
While many-hued shadows glide on the
　　　streets!

(*Balagonda arrives, swinging his arms*)

BALAGONDA:　I don't understand what happened or why.
Even if I pinch myself, it feels like I'm
　　　pinching someone else.
When is the daybreak? When can we see
　　　ourselves?
This is my home, but you know how afraid
　　　I am?
This shed, these cattle, I've never seen them
　　　in the daylight, really.
If I could get a mirror now, I wonder what I'd
　　　look like!

GOWDTI:　Memories flow like kohl down my cheeks,
I search and smell the old blanket
Seeking that same old scent!
Twin serpents appear in my dreams—
How they play, couple and writhe,
Ploughing deep furrows in the earth!

BALAGONDA:　Ayyooo, what's this under my feet?
My feet grow cold, they are melting;
My waist is melting too, my face is coming
　　　off loose!
Looks like in this night I'm floating

All over the house on a raft.
But who is that someone who stands in that
    raft?
And sits down again, who's that now?
Is that me? Am I searching
For this same person who is over there?

GOWDTI: I flow like sweat on these fields,
What's raw blends with other things raw.
Aye, Shiva, my body begins to thrill!
Sprouts come up, and on every shoot,
I see a perching bird.
They chirp and chirp, all the time
But when I open my eyes, what's here?
Ayya Shiva, the wretched old night again!

BALAGONDA: A female voice, a voice I have heard before,
A voice that I hear again and again in my
    heart—
In my heart within which this voice was born.
Are my roots shaking and throbbing? Whose
    voice is this?
Is she the girl who gave me milk and took my
    chain away?

(*Excited. Starts enacting Kamali's meeting with him*)

I got you, sonny Balagonda! White horse,
Silk turban, and a soft smile playing
Under that tender moustache
Aren't you the one who drank
From my pot of milk, gave me the chain,
And went away from here?

GOWDTI: I must bite, I must nibble, I must hug you hard
Like a parrot hanging from a fruit tree,

I'll swing and pull you down to me;
Make love till your bones ache,
Come to me, my love!
I, your beloved, stand here; come and storm
    me now!

BALAGONDA: On the day Balagonda came here, you were
    walking
With a pot of milk; aren't you that girl?
I knew this—that one day or the other I'd
    find you,
That you'd come here for sure!
Won't you look at me? I kept searching to
    catch,
Yes, to catch that man who drank your milk.
He who gave the chain?
He eluded me all these days . . .
So, I wanted you. If you came
And stood here, well, I knew that he'd
Smell the sweat of your thighs and surface
    here too!
Didn't it turn out to be true now?
We found him, didn't we? Now, let that
    Sutradhara
Come and ask me my name!
I'll touch my two-stranded waistband
And swear on it aloud,
Son, if you ask what my name is . . .

GOWDTI: Has your whore collapsed with fatigue?
Come, my king, my man, my hero!
I'll melt like butter in your arms, wherever
    you touch.
Think I'm a piece of chicken—

Come bite my lips and chin!
Maul them, and I'll cry out in my dream.
Mava, my lover, mava, come!

BALAGONDA: Che, I am not the Gowda, can't you see?
With flaming eyes, the bull—
Why is it roaming here? Why do you stand
    so far away?
Come closer to me. By the way, I only
Found out the other day that your name's
    Kamali.
You know how I searched and longed for
    you?
Didn't I tell you then? That I'd find
    Balagonda
In some corner where you and I meet?
Now, if you want, you can ask me
How many letters there are in anyone's
    name—
Not only in mine and yours, but ask me the
    address and identity
Of all these people who sit here, I'll answer
    in a trice!
See for yourself, cut my heart open, hold a
    light,
And check. In every corner there's only your
    name!
When you stood there and sang
It seemed like the song sank into me,
Into the depths of my being—what do you
    say to this?

(*The Gowdti starts singing. But Balagonda continues
to talk*)

BALAGONDA: You know whom I thought of
                The moment the yakshi gave me the gem?
                The gem? It's not just a gem—it's really a
                     charm that can bring us rain!
                So, I sent Laksmya to your house to check
                If you were in or not. I asked him to find out
                If you'd call me home. That . . . son . . . he
                     isn't back yet.
                But okay, you're here now. This gem . . .

(*He holds his head and becomes frantic*)

                Gem? Where's the gem? Avva . . .!

(*He runs inside. You can hear him talking*)

                I am asking . . . where's the gem? Where's
                     everyone?
                Are they dead or what? Avva?

(*The Gowdti enters, shaking her tresses. Balagonda
stands in front of her*)

BALAGONDA: Avva, where's my gem?

(*The Gowdti just stands there looking at him*)

BALAGONDA: Where's Old Gowda?

(*Without waiting for an answer, he runs outside. The
Gowdti slowly disappears. Equally slowly, the sutradhara
appears on the stage*)

SUTRADHARA: Balagonda freed the golden horse in haste . . .
                He sat on it . . . he held the reins . . .
                And rode the horse away . . . Mother, what'll
                     happen to this village?

What'll happen to me? From now on, who
    will bring
The holy offering to you? Who'll celebrate
    your feast?
Where did the Gowda run away?
Where did Balagonda run off?

(*The three deities appear*)

DEITY 2:   Boy, if you come to know what'll happen
          next,
          You'll be even more terrified; why do you
          want to see that?

SUTRADHARA: Then, is there no hope or luck for us?

DEITY 2:   If you are that impatient, come follow me . . .

(*She circles the stage once. We see the outcaste Pari sitting
on the straw bed chewing betel leaves and nuts*)

SUTRADHARA: Ada! Why have we come to the outcaste
          neighbourhood?
          It's so late, why is someone sitting on the
          straw bed at this hour?!
          Shall I talk to this woman for a bit?

(*Deity 2 indicates that he could. The three disappear*)

          Who? Who's this? The outcaste Pari?

PARI: Whoever recognizes an old toothless whore?
          Why would they?
          Why should I fault you for that?

SUTRADHARA: At a time when ghosts glide about,
          If you sit alone here like this,

How should I recognize you, you tell me
    now?
What's more, you truly are the devil
    incarnate!
If all the others vow one thing,
You vow something else.
Tell me, in this darkness,
Why do you sit alone? What's your story?
You look all colourful, chewing betel leaves;
And you wear kohl in your eyes too.
Although you're old, you're still a tart, hey!

PARI: Paraboo, how do I look today?

SUTRADHARA: Shall I say, as good as you can?

PARI: Heyee, tell me!

SUTRADHARA: But I told you . . .

PARI: I'm so excited and so happy today!

SUTRADHARA: What? I don't know the head or tail of what
    You're talking about. How should I know
    Why you are so excited, so happy?

PARI: Hoy, you are . . . forget it!
    Have you seen my daughter, Kamali?

SUTRADHARA: Of course, I have. Just the other day
    She was going off with a pot of milk
    To shower Goddess Karevva's idol . . .

PARI: Hoy, hoy, yes.
    Didn't Balagonda come that day?
    The same day, I gave my daughter
    A potful of milk

And told her, 'Daughter, go shower Karevva's
    idol.'
She said, 'Yes, Mother!'
On the way, it seems, she saw a rider on a
    white horse.
He came at dusk, drank all the milk in the pot;
Then gave her a pearl necklace, a token of
    recognition.
The girl, who went singing, came back crying
She told me this tale only later though.
The whole day, she didn't speak.
Nothing, she said nothing, asked nothing;
Just pressed the chain of pearls to her bosom
    and cried!
You know, when my daughter became a
    woman,
Evil eyes fell on her; the fire that raged
In her body took three days to subside.
But even then, she wasn't this depressed.
God, you know how she was before all this?
Yav, yav, yav . . . she'd cry like a parrot,
Running in and out of the house!
All the neighbourhood whores
Had to touch the ground
And crack their knuckles to ward off the evil
    eye!
This same Old Gowda, if he came home,
Would kiss the child noisily
Even if she'd gone to sleep.
What should I feel if my playful little
Daughter suddenly stops being like that?

SUTRADHARA: Yes, you'd feel so, yes!

PARI: I wondered, 'Goddess of the Hill,
                    What's your wish? Didn't you get my offering?
                    Are you angry with me
                    Because I stopped dancing?
                    I stopped because I have no strength in my
                         feet
                    To dance that dance
                    On the upcoming Wife's Full Moon Day.'
                    I vowed I'd take Kamali to Ellavva's hill.
                    Three days passed, three nights too—
                    Finally, she opened her mouth,
                    And I heard the real story from her!
                    That night, in my dream,
                    A tender boy came—with red braids this
                         long. (*Indicates with her hands*)
                    He wore the sun in his hair
                    He came here with a jasmine-white laugh!

SUTRADHARA: Adadada!

PARI: Yes, even if one word of what I've said
                    Isn't true, let the Goddess of the Hill punish
                         me!
                    He came this Monday morning,
                    Showed me the chain and said,
                    He'd throw the bhandara on the vermilion
                    Which adorned my daughter's forehead then.
                    Then, he just disappeared!
                    Avva, Goddess of the Hill, Ellavva,
                    Karimari Karevva, Lagumavva of the gorge,
                    Niravani of the Hills—and all the other gods!
                    You see, I got up sweating hard;
                    My body thrilled and stank like the raw red
                         earth.

I got up and saw my daughter's face;
This wench was mumbling and laughing in
    her sleep!
Avva, Goddess of the Hill,
I wanted to test my dream.
So, on Monday, I put vermilion on my
    daughter's forehead
And sat waiting. As I sat waiting, the servant
    Lasimya came.
The moment he said, 'Balagonda wants to
    come here,
Shall I bring him?' you can imagine what I
    felt!
So, here I was, sitting and chewing betel
    leaves . . .
And there comes Balagonda riding a white
    horse!

SUTRADHARA: Is Balagonda in the house now?

PARI: Yes, why?

SUTRADHARA: Was there a gem on his head?

PARI: How it shone! Ah, like the nose ring of the
    Goddess of the Hill!

SUTRADHARA: How was the horse?

PARI: White. Don't you see it there?

SUTRADHARA: God, I saw Old Gowda mount the white horse
    With my own eyes, what happened!
    Mother . . .

(*He goes to where the deities had appeared earlier. At the
same moment, Balagonda enters*)

BALAGONDA: Is this the house of the outcaste Paravva?

PARI: Hoy, yes! Who's this? Ayya, Ayya!
               You who were inside, how did you appear
                    outside?
               What kind of drama is going on here?

*(As Balagonda tries to enter the house, the sutradhara
runs on the stage, bumps against Balagonda and stops,
amazed)*

SUTRADHARA: Appa, who are you?
               Holding a sickle in your hand, you come
                    riding the red horse.
               What is your good name?

BALAGONDA: Have you no sense of time or propriety?
               Asking me my name now! Let me go . . .

*(Inside, Kamali screams suddenly. Balagonda looks
afraid for a moment. Then, he comes to a decision and
runs inside, holding his sickle. 'Catch him, catch that
thief! Hey, Son, hey!' we hear him shouting inside.
Old Gowda runs from one end of the stage to the other
with his shirt and turban stuck under his armpit.
Balagonda chases him, shouting. We know that they have
gone further away as his voice recedes. Kamali enters,
screaming like a crazy woman, and hugs her mother.
At this very moment, Pari is possessed by Ellavva. She
scrunches her eyes and starts dancing on the stage in a
terrible manner, then moves backstage. Kamali looks
all around her helplessly. Then, disappointed, she faints.
All the three deities who had appeared earlier reappear
now, along with the sutradhara on the fore-stage. The
sutradhara salutes them)*

SUTRADHARA: Mother, don't fold this secret into your fist
       and hide it
From our eyes. What's the underlying
       meaning of all this?
Please solve this riddle for us.
True, Old Gowda took the gem; true that he
Mounted the white horse too;
Who was the other Balagonda then?

DEITY 2:   Sutradhara, Old Gowda took
The gem and came to Kamali's house
In Balagonda's form.
When Balagonda realized what he'd lost
And started looking for it, he came across the
       servant, Lasimya.
Wondering, Lasimya asked, 'You were in
       Pari's house,
How did you come here?' Then Lasimya
       started running away,
Thinking that Balagonda was a ghost. But
       Balagonda held him
And asked what happened.
Then he found his way to Pari's house
And came here;
Child, do you recognize me at least now?

SUTRADHARA: Mother, we all know that you're Lagumavva.
But big people like you, how come you're here?
Out of your temple, and here in the open?
Do let us know.

DEITY 2:   We too have been orphaned like you!
We're waiting for some hero, from some
       corner of the world

To arrive here and save us from this fate.
Sutradhara, look, there, some people are
    dancing
Around a fire, why? There are three heaps in
    the middle.
What're those now? And why do they sing?

SUTRADHARA: Oh, that? That's an old ritual to bring rain
Three good wives of the village
Go together and get the black cow's dung
They're now burning three dung cakes there.
If in three days and three nights,
Worms surface in those dung heaps,
It'll rain.
Today is the new moon. In the morning—
The end of this period—we'll make Pari
Pray and pick in there for worms.
All the villagers have gathered there for this.
Okay, it's now time for sunrise,
I too will go and see what fate holds for us.
If there are no worms, we'll all go away
    together
To someplace else.

THREE DEITIES: If that happens, Sutradhara, we'll go with
    you too.

SUTRADHARA: (*Saluting*) All right, Mothers! You can come
    with us too.

(*All exit. The sutradhara also leaves. From far away, you
hear the familiar song 'Rain, rain, pour away' indistinctly.
The dancing Pari suddenly stops and screams, 'Mother,
protect us! Save us, Rama!' The curtain falls even as she
is saying this*)

Act IV

(The sutradhara and the people sing.)

Rain, rain, pour away
Pour away on this day!
You who said you'd be back soon
Where're you? And when will you come?
The earth is cracked, touched by the
Netherworld's hot breath,
The word 'green' is gone!
The body of our weeping earth is dry.
You forgot the fire in your loins, Rain God!
Please send us showers to flood that
      netherworld too.
Lakes and wells are dry, there're just three
      drops of water
Now, there is only the shadow of a single star
      here
Great big streams are dry bathrooms,
Young fish have nothing to eat!
Our skins are like black blankets.
We wander, doing the Guruchiya ritual, Rain
      God[7]

81

Please send us showers to flood that
netherworld too.

*(They sing and dance. Later, some of them warm
themselves by the fire, smoking the pipe or chewing
tobacco. They sit anywhere and anyhow. In the beginning,
they talk without bothering about who's listening. Nobody
seems to care. Later, when they realize that someone is
eavesdropping, they scratch their bodies in embarrassment)*

GURYA: Hasn't the morning broken yet?

ERIPYA: The cockerel crowed, didn't he?

GURYA: Even though the cockerel crowed, the
                morning hasn't broken.

YAMANYA: The sun has risen, right?

GURYA: Everything needed to make
                The morning break has happened; we've
                    yawned,
                Rubbed our eyes, stretched our bodies . . .

ELYA: Let the morning break when it wants to,
                What's the hurry? God knows
                What all awaits us now!

GURYA: And even that which has to surface hasn't
                surfaced?

ERIPYA: Some who wanted to know about this went to
                The outcaste neighbourhood, some to the
                    cemetery;
                Others to the Gowda's house—didn't he tell
                    you?
                I knew that this path doesn't take us anywhere;

It'll only take us to the cemetery.
Didn't you see, the other day? The girl
    who left in the morning, to throw the
    cowdung out,
Found herself in the village cemetery!

YAMANYA: Ghosts from everywhere seem to have
    gathered here, Appa!
The other day, it seems, some ghost that
    looked like Old Gowda
Waved and called out thrice to my wife!
What do you do? Thank God, she's gutsy!
'Ramagonda,' she cried out thrice, the ghost
    vanished.
But the ghost took its revenge on our
    pregnant buffalo,
That son of a bitch! The same Gowda had
    once asked,
'300 rupees, I'll count and throw that amount
    on this black blanket;
Give me that buffalo.' Who knew his next
    plan though?
The buffalo, which had gone to graze, never
    came back at all.

GURYA: Have the worms surfaced in the dung?

ELYA: Don't you have anything else to talk about?

GURYA: By the way, the day before yesterday,
In Gokak, it seems there occurred a rain of
    blood.
In some village, the watchman got up
In the middle of the night and saw a shower
    of burning cinders!

He scrunched his eyes in fear and never
    opened them again.

ERIPYA: In short, it is a mistake to be born.

GURYA: Will they surface?

ELYA: Hey, you are back to singing the same song?

GURYA: It seems he got Parisya killed . . .

ERIPYA: Who? Who? That old man?

ELYA: Ah ha, acts like he knows nothing!

ERIPYA: True, I know all this. But even if I hear it a
        hundred times
    I'll want to again and again. But when I do,
    I feel as if I am dead. Crazy, right? By the way,
        how did you say he died?

GURYA: Parisya went to Old Gowda and asked:
    'Sir, please let your bull cross my cow.'
    Old Gowda let the bull do its job
    And asked for two rupees. This
    son Parisya . . . he screamed, saying,
    'No, I won't!'

ERIPYA: Isn't that wrong on Parisya's part?

GUDYA: Hey, don't start judging before you know
        things.
    If the bull crosses the cow properly
    You should pay two rupees, that's correct.
    But if it just sniffs and sticks its chin in?

ERIPYA: You're right. Does he think we are
    Like the vegetables in his field or what?

He will let us be if he wants, if not
He will cut our heads, is that it?

GURYA: Man, when Parisya died, I felt like I'd died too.
If the village is so full of sin
Do you think what should surface in the dung
Will surface at all?

ELYA: You know? I saw the Nandi pillar break in my
dream.

YAMANYA: And in my dream? Listen, I'll tell you, Appa!
Some old man held the sky in his hand
And shook it like this . . .
The stars fell, tumbling down to the earth.

ERIPYA: Maybe this oldie will croak!

GURYA: He who shakes the sky up?
How will he die, man?

YAMANYA: Only Pari knows such things.
Has nobody gone to get Pari yet? Go, Seepya.
She must wake up and get ready for the
prayer.
Go, you go!

(*Seepya gets up, looking scared*)

You speak big, but are you a man?
Why are you so scared to go?
If you feel afraid, keep singing on your way.

(*Seepya leaves. Shouting to him*)

When she brings the holy water for worship,
Don't let anyone touch or pollute it.

Bring her here carefully. If someone touches that water,
It brings bad luck to the village. You must know this . . .

(Yamanya starts talking to the other people on the stage in a lower voice)

She can interpret all kinds of things;
What's this little matter to her?
I say that she'll say something about all this;
What do you say?

GURYA: Do you think they will surface if she says something?

YAMANYA: You don't think they will?

GURYA: Why not?

ELYA: Your father's balls—You are still very young, why do you want to know all this?
We grit our teeth and sit still.
Don't you know what to ask and what not? What do you eat for food?
Grass or something? They'll surface if they want to;
Won't if they don't want to.
Who'll snatch our luck from us? If we are lucky, how can
The Gowda's sin hurt us? How can our own sins hurt us? What, Appa?

GURYA: So, you think it's all a matter of luck?

YAMANYA: What else?

ERIPYA: I have lost faith in luck; what if it is bad?

YAMANYA: No, no. Are you trying to scare us by saying our luck is bad?
I didn't even get scared when my wife saw me scratching
The herpes in my groin; will I feel scared by your words?

ERIPYA: Go, go away, you low life! You don't even have the guts
To beat your wife in the streets during daylight.
You want to talk now, do you?
I know you well, go away!

ELYA: How did you know that our luck was bad? Your tender stomach
Can't even digest butter. You talk big things now, hey?
We must skin such people alive and hang them up.

YAMANYA: Man, because of this fellow, didn't my wife scold me,
Saying I have become an empty bag?

ERIPYA: Yeey, I'll tell you, okay? Listen,
It is true that our luck is bad; in these dung heaps . . .

ELYA: (*Interrupting him*)
I will fold my hands, salute you, and drag my bum off from here!
As it is, the outcaste Pari was saying that we are seeing whores and widows

Everywhere in the village; on top of all that,
    we have this now!
That word shouldn't fall on my ears, God!
I sleep to forget it, but the morning breaks
    again;
Evening again, and then morning again . . .
Why is your face green?

ERIPYA: Why would my face look green? Shut up, man!
Seems you see whores and widows! Shall I
    tell you
Why my wife looks like a whore-widow?
    Why do
You hide things? I know what Pari told you.
    Shall I tell you now?
Look, everybody! The other day, I was
    standing in the river to bathe;
The outcaste Ningi had hitched her saree up
    her thighs,
And was washing clothes.
At some point, her saree slipped away; she
    quickly snuck behind a rock there.
I turned my face away. Then she stood up
    revealing everything and challenged me,
'Can't you even whistle, you low life?!'
Being a decent chap, I didn't say a word.
She draped her saree back quickly, ate betel
    leaves,
Looked at me and spat thrice. I remained
    quiet even then.
'Should I think you are a cow, or should I
    think you are a butcher?'
I said, 'Think I am a cow.' 'Your wife has
    become a whore-widow,

Go see!' she cursed. Then, she went away!
    She has gossiped with Pari.
Pari has carried the tale to this fellow; now
    he comes here,
And throws up all this stuff. How am I to
    blame for anything?

GURYA: Who'll sleep on the same old bed all day? Tell
    me, my son!

YAMANYA: We all are worried about the rains; she is
    worrying about paramours!

ELYA: What else does she know, except the sleeping
    mattress and a paramour next her?

ERIPYA: Did I say something wrong?

ELYA: Hey, hey, don't say anything . . . you son!
    I know who you are.
What if there is someone else's name in your
    schoolbooks,
Your real father's name is written all over
    your face, man!
Ask your mother this . . .
Who gave her the chain of little gold bells
    that she wears on her neck?
Talk to me after that, I'll accept whatever you
    say!

ERIPYA: You want to teach me, hey? I'll smash your
Bones . . . you son! What about your story?
    Just because you
Don't even know your father, you keep asking
    the outcaste
Kamali, 'Do you know who I am?'

At least we know our fathers' names. If we
forget those,
At least we can mention Old Gowda's name
shamelessly. What do you have?
You who talk with that boneless tongue, you
bloody lech!
I'll pull your moustache out and hand it to
you, be careful!

ELYA: Hey, who's a lech?

GURYA: What do you care? Shut up. This bastard has a
Pustule on his penis. His words also stink like
that pustule.

ELYA: What pustule? What pustule?

GURYA: The other day, he saw himself in the mirror
and asked his wife,
'The man in the mirror doesn't look like me.
Who's he?'
His wife told him,
'There are so many in the village;
Think that it's any one of those!'
He's taking out that frustration on us now,
the son of a bitch!

ERIPYA: Hey, whom are you calling a son of a bitch,
you . . . son!
Have you been an eyewitness to my mother's
whoring or what?
Let's settle the scores today. Who cares if the
worms surface in the dung heaps
Or not? If they do, we'll stay back in the
village; if not, we'll leave.

(*Others try to stop him. But he stands up and keeps talking*)

> We'll settle this today; I'll drink your blood today, you oldie without balls!

(*He jumps on Gurya and tries to strangle him. Everybody tries to separate them and make them stand apart but fail. There is confusion on the stage. Now, the old man who sits unnoticed in the corner suddenly screams. He is the same old man whom Balagonda had met in Act II. The old man has smeared a lot of bhandara on his forehead and has fully covered himself with a blanket. He has a flask in his hand. He shrieks like someone possessed*)

OLD MAN: Yeyee . . . yeyeee . . . (*Everybody becomes silent*) The worms will surface in the dung heap . . . you son!

(*People hold his arm reverently, bring him to the fore-stage, make him sit, and settle down around him*)

ELYA: See, he speaks of worms with no fear at all!

GURYA: See if he has been possessed by a devil or something!

ERIPYA: (*To Gurya*) Stay quiet, Appa! He speaks like a God in a temple;
Shut up for a bit and listen;
Speak, speak on, old man!

ELYA: I say that we should put him in the temple and worship him,
What do you say? Don't you see? His words fall Like a jasmine shower. Speak, old man, speak!

OLD MAN: I have nobody to call my own now . . . ancient
     old man—
     I am as old as an eagle. This is the time when
     You sit with your head stuck between your
      knees, right?
     But even when I sit so, why shouldn't I think
      I'm still young?
     If you do, you must look deep within!
     So, I asked the sages, then the *sharanas*,[8]
     And *siddhas*. Finally, on the Nirvanappa hill,
     Our Goddess, Parembi Karevva, came in the
      guise of
     Pari and gave me something, saying, 'Drink
      this, my son.'
     I drank it, and you know what happened?
     Youth all over my body! My arms are young,
     My legs are young—I'm fully young!
     Then, with a tender smile under a budding
      moustache,
     Wearing a turban poised stylishly on his head
     Comes this hero on a white horse!
     I look at him and wonder, 'Who is this?'
     It's me! Young girls bearing milk pots
     Keep calling me on the streets,
     Elbowing each other and saying, 'Maama,[9]
     Drink my milk,' and 'Drink my milk, Maama!'

YAMANYA: Hey, Grandpa, give me some too!

(*When the old man gives him the flask, he puts it to his
lips and drinks. At the same time, another person stretches
his hand out for it. Yamanya passes it on and salutes it,
folding his hands. The other too salutes the flask once when
he takes it, and again when he passes it on to the next*

person. When everyone has drunk, conversation begins.
Everyone acts drunk from now onwards)

OLD MAN: Look, people! Why shouldn't we imagine
              that the worms
              Have surfaced in those dung heaps?

YAMANYA: What a significant point you've raised, my appa!
              Why only worms? Tell me what all we should
                  imagine!
              Worms have surfaced in the dung heaps . . .
                  rain splashes,
              The crop grows instantly—up to the knee, to
                  the waist,
              Up to the chest; sprouts come up bright, like
                  the Gowdti's face;
              Little grains stick to them like her nose ring;
              The palms sway in the breeze like her saree's
                  seragu!
              Aha . . . Grandpa, you tell us again;
              Only you speak; speak on!

ELYA: The drink has descended to my neck now.

GURYA: It has dropped to my chest now.

ERIPYA: It has flowed to my knees.

OLD MAN: Strapping young girls bearing their milk pots
              Keep calling out to me again and again,
                  'Maama, drink my milk!
              Maama, drink my milk! How much did you
                  drink?'

GURYA: How well you speak, old man,
              Like you know everything!

	You sound like a God, my dear old man!

ELYA: How well you talk! Really, how well!
I want to call you my grandpa;
Almost want to call you my father sometimes!
I feel such a surge of affection for you, what
    do I do?
Whether you say yes or no, before I die
I'll call you that once!
I have never cheated on anybody but my wife,
    okay?
Yes, that same outcaste Sita;
When she begged me for a cheap bauble,
I sold half my field and gave her half a seer's
    measure of gold—
That's the kind of man I am, a real man!
The chain got so heavy for her neck that
    she'd fall at my feet
And at every step, call me, 'Maama . . .'
Ask this fellow if you want; isn't this true,
    man?

ERIPYA: Feels like someone is tickling my armpit and
    making me laugh.
Come, let's enact a play; you become the
    whore, Chimana!

YAMANYA: Ah, my dear! What illusions, do you hear?

GURYA: It seems that the world was born yesterday,
    and we just now.
Ha, what a world! What a world!

(*Pari enters bearing a pot. She looks at these people, and
is surprised*)

PARI: Ay, Shiva! What are these fools doing?
You'll pollute the pot, get out of my way!

ELYA: Arre, the girl with the milk pot is here!
She is waylaying me! Maama, drink my milk,
Drink my milk.

(*He starts chasing Pari. The others chase her too, chanting,
'Maama, drink my milk, drink my milk!' She circles the
stage twice and tries to escape*)

YAMANYA: Look, she's like a sugar doll!

ERIPYA: (*Catching her*) Look, she's become a dollop of butter!

(*Pari frees her hand from someone who is holding it, spits
on his face, and runs away. The others go after her, yelling,
'Drink my milk! Drink my milk!' Only the sutradhara
and the old man remain on the stage*)

OLD MAN: What? What did you say?

SUTRADHARA: Appa, I have no idea. Everything looks
the same to my dull brain! Why did you
ask me?

OLD MAN: If Balagonda comes and asks after me now,
tell him
I'm in the forest in the north. What'll you say?

(*Old Gowda says this and leaves. The sutradhara
addresses the audience*)

SUTRADHARA: Young lad!
There's a red sea in the south;
In the red sea, there's a green rock in the
middle;

On that rock in the middle, there's a dense
   forest,
And in the forest there's a colourful palace.
In front of the palace a big eagle sits,
In one of his talons he holds a golden scale
and a gun in the other.
He hunts four thousand species of victims
Outside the palace, and he rules there.
You go there and meet him now.

Act V

SUTRADHARA: Our father, hear us please!
Where did my brother go, where is he?
I'll fold my hands, I'll fall at your feet;
Don't kill us for nothing!
The colour has melted from our lives,
And we glide like shadows
Not me, not the other!
Drowning in this loss of self,
A fool who knows not the past;
What do I know of the future?
I seek that Guru who knows,
He, who will give me that knowledge.
Until then, keep me from harm, my God!

(*The sutradhara's song ends and 'Laalima Dhruva' is heard for a long time. The moment this starts, we see Balagonda entering with a sickle. Old Gowda enters too, from the opposite side. Until 'Laalima Dhruva' ends, Balagonda keeps staring at the Gowda, as if searching for something in his face. The Gowda twirls his moustache and laughs. When Balagonda finds what he is looking for, he doesn't seem happy. In the end, Balagonda's face looks*

97

like that of a corpse, but Old Gowda's face glows with new
lustre. His laugh and attitude are strangely attractive)

BALAGONDA: Like flint stones about to spark off—
We met, I got you today. Come, my friend!
To catch, catch you, how much I have searched;
I've been sharpening my sickle for a very long
time!
Still, now that I've found you, I won't kill you
right away.
Because, you see, I have a couple of words to
say.
What, Appa? If I were to kill you right here
right now,
Then who'll answer my questions? Tell me, sir!
Perhaps, it wouldn't have mattered if it were
something else,
But certain matters are different, right?
They're important, right?
Yes, they are. Now, you must listen to me!
You know why? Because, it's only you
Who knows the challenge that lurks behind
my speech.
I've dug into my heart and groped for an
answer.
After all the fatigue, there's some strange
relief!
What, Appa? So, where should I catch you?
When? When you're talking? When you're
whoring?
I hold this sickle, and I can think of as many
tricks
To catch you as the beatings of my pulse.

If I tried those tricks just to get this audience's
    applause,
Will I get what I want?
No. Often, we want something but what
    happens is something else!
Just know this, old man! The other day, this
    Sutradhara asked me,
'What's your name?' But before I could reply,
Like neighbours getting out to fight,
Ten or fifteen came out from within me.
They started telling everybody their names!
I don't know the name of even one of them.
    Which butcher is this?
What fire demon is that other? How did they
    all exist within me
Without me even knowing about them? But
    then, what's my real name?
If I have to utter my name in front of all these
    people,
And if I have to know what that name is . . .
    I'll have to kill someone like you.
What, Appa? Ask me why, and I'll tell you.

OLD GOWDA: Whatever it is that's troubling you . . . why
    don't you ask it to yourself?

BALAGONDA: (*As if he didn't hear him*)
    The other day, when I was half asleep,
    I dreamt a scary dream!
    I had shut the door of the house
    And closed the windows too;
    It looked like a well gaped in the hallway,
    And the netherworld opened up within it.
    I stood there looking—

Someone came and slapped me on the back
I turned around to see. Ah, a beautiful
　　　Goddess!
'Mother!' I was about to cry, but I woke up.
No gem! You took it and went to Pari's house;
I found that out later!
I felt angry with you . . . but also felt
Like calling out and congratulating you!
On that day, at midnight,
I had planned to go to Kamali's house.
I locked up, sent Lasimya to see if she was in,
And sat waiting. Then I felt a bit sleepy,
When I lay down there, you took my form,
Took my gem, and went there first, right?
That was very smart, wasn't it?
So that day I decided
That I could make a name for myself
Only if I killed you.
Why do you laugh like that?

OLD GOWDA:　　Brother, you survive only because you have
　　　　　　　　that big mouth.
How much you talk and talk! I've been
　　　watching
Since this play began—you keep yap, yap,
　　　yapping,
Like a frog croaking away to glory.
You just don't let go, wherever I go.

BALAGONDA:　　Old man, whatever a warrior says, it sounds
　　　　　　　　like
The sharpening of a sickle.

OLD GOWDA:　　Nothing to cut, nothing to slash . . .

What's the point of sharpening the sickle, tell
    me that?
Since I was born I have killed all the people
I have wanted to kill, but even my right hand
Doesn't know what my left hand did.
If one could kill only with one's talk,
The butcher's pet parrot would
Have become a minister in this land!
Fool, head back home and light the lamp;
Look at the shadow on the wall;
Go cut that up! Che! I have begun
To feel great pity for you, my boy!
Partly because you are my real son
And partly because you are such a sickly
    fellow!

BALAGONDA: Do you think I'll still believe such lies?
You are a demon—you turned into a tiger
And you killed my father. You took his form
And ruled the village—you think I don't
Know all this?

OLD GOWDA: Great, great! You know a lot!
Really, a lot! The schoolmaster
Should bow down to you for your knowledge!
Why do you say things which make me want
    to clap and laugh?
Balagonda, actually that demon . . .

BALAGONDA: Look now, don't speak your name and mine
    in the same breath!

OLD GOWDA: There he goes again!
These words are not befitting you, Brother!
You learn to speak differently now.

Look, there's a eunuch in Pari's house
You train with him for a few days;
He'll teach you how to carry the water pot,
How to swing your arms like a woman,
How to dance on the hill on Ellamma's new-
    moon and full-moon feasts.[10]
Or how to win a man—he'll teach you
    everything.
Thoo! Instead of giving birth to you
Shouldn't your mother have laid a fart as big
    as you?
At least a few people would have stopped
    their noses!

BALAGONDA: Old man, old man!
You're trying to be over-smart.

OLD GOWDA: When I saw the spirit with which you came
    to kill me
I felt so happy! After all, the seed is mine!
Even if I die by your hand, like the lizard's spit
I wanted to grow inside, secretly, over
    generations in the village people's wombs.
I wanted, when I died, to create a poem and
    sing, 'Even if I die, the new moon
Will always come, my son!' I wanted to fly
    and shimmer like a flag . . .
These were my dreams! But you weren't born
    to men like me—
You were born to mere words! Killing is not
    mouthing words
It should be in your blood.
You write these words in your heart, but
    know this much:

There's no flesh or blood in you; no, no!
There's only the spittle of sickly men.
Go away! He tries to show off, aha; show off
    his valour!

BALAGONDA: Old man, you are trying to fill yourself
By emptying me!

OLD GOWDA: Shut up, hey! What's lacking in me that
I should fill myself with what's yours?
In all your life, you wouldn't have eaten
As much as I have thrown up in one go!
Sonny, you were born the day before
And opened your eyes only yesterday;
Today, he comes to donate all his riches to
    me!
Get out, you low life! If you see a fruit in a
    picture—
Your mouth begins to water; but you can't eat
    it, right?
Go, stand like the whetting-stone
At the edge of that village stream.
Women who come and go
To fetch water from there,
Can sharpen their looks on you.

BALAGONDA: Old man, you're speaking my words . . .

OLD GOWDA: Why, yes! Yes, of course yes!
Why not, yes? What'll you do anyway?
You began Kamali's initiation
Into her profession, but I ate the fruit!
They gave the gem to you,
But I stole that! At every step, I've challenged
Your strength. I'm not just a man of words—

Oh, but I'm so upset that I bore a son like
    you!
One day, I planned on telling this Paribya
    here
That Balagonda is my son.
But I won't do it now;
Go die without a father's name.

BALAGONDA: (*Screams*) Old man . . .!

OLD GOWDA: The nerve in your neck will snap!
Why do you scream like that? You can't even
    quarrel
Well enough to make a few people say,
'Aha, he's something for us to reckon with!'
Look, I'll take this turban that real men wear,
And this sickle doesn't suit your arm like
    women's bangles do!
So, I'll take that sickle too . . .

(*He snatches the turban and sickle, pats Balagonda on his
back and continues*)

Look, I'm taking all of these—
What'll you do about it? I'll say a word of
    advice, though,
Leave off your old ways!

(*Old Gowda turns to leave. Immediately, Balagonda
plants his hands on the Gowda's chest and pushes him*)

BALAGONDA: You're my father, right?

OLD GOWDA: Why do you ask?

BALAGONDA: Tell me if it's true.

OLD GOWDA: Will you cry if I don't tell you?
You'll get the answer only when you know
    your father.
Not by talking, singing and crying.
If I keep standing before you,
You'll tell me another story,
Like some silly balladeer
Go home now, get going!
Go clever little boy!

(*Like one consoles a child, he caresses Balagonda's chin, mocking him*)

BALAGONDA: My turban, gem and sickle—give them back
    to me, quick . . .!

(*Old Gowda dances around Balagonda, mocking him, as seen in the open-air folk play Bayalata. Balagonda keeps screaming the same words, 'Please give it back! Give, Appa . . .' The old man turns to leave without bothering about this. Even as he is screaming, Balagonda is searching for a stone. When he finds a big enough stone, he hurls it at Old Gowda. Old Gowda starts to scream in pain, acting like a mad man; Balagonda is taken aback. Eventually, after letting out a moan or two, Old Gowda dies*)

BALAGONDA: Now you know, right? Didn't I show you?
I did it, right?

(*Saying this, he takes the old man's turban and places it on his own head. He also takes the gem and the sickle, stuffs Old Gowda's body in a bag, slings it on his shoulder, and leaves*)

BALAGONDA: Sutradhara!

SUTRADHARA: Yes?

BALAGONDA: What's on my back?

SUTRADHARA: The bundle of old karma.

BALAGONDA: I'll throw this in the dry well outside the
               village
               Bathe and get back.
               Meanwhile, tell the outcaste Kamali
               To come and wait for me on the grazing
                    platform
               Of our cattle-shed.

SUTRADHARA: I'll tell her, you please go.

  (*'Laalima Dhruva' can be heard. Balagonda exits*)

SUTRADHARA: (*Singing the song of the Earth Woman who
               longs for love and rain*)
               I hope fervently, I long for so many things,
               Show me some mercy, come, my beloved
                    Mohana!
               The jasmine blossom is in bloom
               And here is its heady scent,
               You smelled it once, and your hand itched—
               To touch those flowers, didn't it, my king!
               Come, drape me like the cloth next to your
                    skin—
               My rich friend, my hero, my king!
               I shed my shyness, my shame, and my honour
               And became fully naked then
               I remember that now, I make my body a
                    temple
               I dig into my stomach to hide your secret
                    there!

And I thrill, when I think of that, ah, I thrill,
　　my king!
You know not what you do, you babble too
　　much,
Why commit this pollution of speech?
That's a spittle-like life, ha, King!
You forget, you stumble, and search for
　　something
That you can hold in your words
You are lost in doubt,
And you forget the body, you forget the truth
　　of the body, my king!
Is the touch on the skin, or the skin lost in
　　touch?
That awareness of you and me,
Flares up like the spark from the flint stones
But we came ridden with this curse,
The curse that cannot be lifted, my king!

(*When the sutradhara's song is halfway through,
Balagonda enters wearing Old Gowda's clothes. He moves
in the background. The song is over. The sutradhara
leaves. Balagonda looks infinitely tired. He comes and
sits on the platform on the stage. The audience hears
many excited voices coming from a distance; they slowly
get louder and become more distinct. Suddenly, Kamali
enters, looking excited*)

KAMALI:　　　Rain, rain, it's raining, folks!
　　　　　　It blew in here; it's drenching us here.
　　　　　　My sweating body, ah, its scent!
　　　　　　See how it smells, hey . . .!
　　　　　　I've never sweated like this.
　　　　　　Look! Look how it pours, hey . . .!

(*She walks up and down the stage, keeps wiping off her perspiration and bustles around excitedly*)

SUTRADHARA: (*Enters joyfully*)
>   Ramagonda! Ramagonda came!
>   He wants to see you
>   Shall I call him in?

(*Balagonda signals a 'no' with his eyes closed. Slowly, he gets up and leaves. People outside cheer loudly, 'Rain, rain, rain!' The sutradhara salutes the audience. The curtain falls*)

MAHMOUD GAWAN

CHARACTERS

Allauddin
Humayun
Begum Nargis
Ahmed Shah
Khwaja Gawan
Neeli/Sapphire
Nizamulmulk
Turk
Panta
Mahar Vitthala
Old man/Chorus
Karim Khan
Khilledar

Servants, soldiers, *tarafdars*, amirs, nobles, commanders,
doorman, messenger, students/tourists (boys and girls)
stranger, citizens, elders, old men and others

PART I

Scene 1

(*A group of six boys and girls, who are tourists from a faraway place, are visiting Bidar's madrasa.*)

BOY 1: If the ruins look like this, imagine what the building would have looked like in its days of glory!

BOY 2: Yes, I have seen the picture of this madrasa as it used to be in those times. It was in our history book. It was just wonderful! And how exciting this place would have been when people actually lived here! Hey, you know what they say about such old monuments? That they whisper in the night . . .

GIRL 1: God, that's scary!

BOY 3: This same madrasa looks marvellous in our history books. But when you see it here . . . why? Why is it like this?

BOY 1: Actually, there should be guides around here to explain all this to us.

GIRL 2: Forget guides, not a soul from the city seems to pass by here!

BOY 2: I suppose people who see this every day don't find it special. Look, someone is coming. We'll ask him, wait. Sir! Hello . . .

STRANGER: (*Stands and looks at them questioningly*) What?

BOY 2: Is there no guide here who can tell us something about this monument, sir?

STRANGER: No. Not if you want someone who knows a lot about this. But do you see that old man sitting there? If you ask him, he will tell you everything about its history. To tell you the truth, he's the only man who can tell you exactly what happened here. In fact, he tells the story like it's all happening right in front of your eyes! I don't think any guide can match him in this!

GIRL 2: If we go to him and ask for information about this building, he'll tell us, won't he?

STRANGER: Yes, go ask him. Though I must warn you, he's a little crazy! Sometimes, he starts imagining that he himself is the diwan of those times. You should bear with this for a bit.

GIRL 3: (*Alarmed*) You mean . . .?

STRANGER: Now, now, don't be so alarmed! While narrating, he gets excited and starts acting like he was right there when all this history happened! You just nod your head and keep saying 'ha' or 'yes', and listen to him quietly. You see, he's the only man who can give you authentic information about all this. He knows secrets lost to history. Suddenly, you'll see him acting like he is Gawan himself. He'll even tell you that he had this madrasa built! If you pretend to believe him a little . . . he's really a lively old man, you know!

GIRL 1: He won't harm us or something, will he?

STRANGER: *Che, che*, he's a good old man. If you want me to, I'll go with you. You don't get bored even if you hear his story a hundred times. Come, let's go.

(*They all go to the old man sitting alone at a distance*)

STRANGER: I salute you, Grandpa! How're you?

OLD MAN: Who are they?

STRANGER: Grandpa, these are college students. They have come to see Bidar. You please tell them something about the history of this place and what happened here.

OLD MAN: I see. What have you come here to know?

GIRL 2: Everything. When was this madrasa built? Who built it? Tell us the story right from the beginning, Grandpa!

OLD MAN: Ha, that's a long story, Little Sister! See, this is a madrasa . . . in its time, there wasn't another educational institution of this calibre on the entire globe! The world's greatest pundits, scientists and astronomers were here! Those thirsty for knowledge came here from all corners of the world! It was well known that the education you got here was not available anywhere else. Even the great Vijayanagar kings didn't have a university like this. A famous traveller of those times declared that this madrasa could put even the grand old Roman institutions of knowledge to shame!

GIRL 3: Then why did that legendary university become like this? Who built it? Who destroyed it? Our history books say that this was built by Mahmoud Gawan, who was the minister, the diwan, at that time. They describe him in glowing terms, saying that he was a splendid scholar, poet, scientist, educationist, politician, philosopher and what not. You tell us about him first.

OLD MAN: Yes! It was the same diwan, whom you described as poet, scientist and so on, who built this madrasa. What's more, he built it with his own money! He'd pay the scholars here out of his salary. Even the king didn't know all this.

BOY 2: They say he came from Iran. Why did he come here?

OLD MAN: Wait, I'll tell you everything! This isn't some 'Once-upon-a-time' type of story, okay? You know, it really happened. A history book is based on facts which historians know. But what I'm going to give you is an eyewitness account! You'll realize this soon enough.

GIRL 1: Right, you start from Mahmoud Gawan.

OLD MAN: Then listen, I'll tell you the story . . . Gawan's uncle was the minister for the king of Iran. Young Gawan helped his uncle in his office. Later, he even became the deputy minister. Although the position wasn't all that important, it gave him a lot of work experience. Many years passed. He became famous for his valour, his administrative acumen and his sharp intellect. At this time, because of some political instability in the kingdom, the whole administrative order crashed. People were distraught. They were turbulent times indeed! Finally, our Gawan left the kingdom with his uncle and went back to his native village. Later, by a strange happenstance, he met our religious guru, Khwaja Kirmani, there. It was Khwaja Kirmani who told Gawan about the great Sufi saint Bande Nawaz. This changed Gawan's life!

Khwaja Kirmani told Gawan, 'Khwaja Bande Nawaz is the greatest saint of our times. He knew God. He travelled across the world, gained a lot of experiences in life, and disseminated his wisdom to all. So, instead of living in a place where people fight over petty things, you go to Hindustan, where Bande Nawaz lived and worked for religious harmony. In Hindustan, people live together with a thousand different faiths and a hundred different philosophies. Despite all this diversity, they respect each other and live in harmony. I think this is the right way to live.'

The moment he heard this, Gawan decided to go to India. He left his wife and children in Iran and set off.

BOY 3: Did he come here directly?

OLD MAN: But he'd need a job to live in India, right? So, he brought a team of horses on the ship to trade. When he got off in Kabola in Ratnagiri district, the administrators of Vijayanagar kingdom went to him and bought all the horses, except two, for a cheap price they set. Later, Gawan came to Gulbarga with the two horses left.

GIRL 2: Gulbarga? Why?

OLD MAN: In this place, Khwaja Bande Nawaz had conducted a famous experiment with Shivalinga Swami of the Savalagi *matha*. Gawan wanted to see this place.

GIRL 1: What experiment was that? We haven't heard of it!

OLD MAN: In a small village called Savalagi in Gulbarga, a young swami treated Hindus and Muslims alike. He tried to bring harmony between these two communities. Bande Nawaz went there and joined the young swami in his endeavours. They became great friends. As a token of their friendship, they swapped clothes. They came up with a new slogan, '*Din Hara Hara*', for their mission of binding the two religions together. Have you young people ever been to the Savalagi matha, the swami's ashram?

BOY 1: Oho, we've seen it. Even went to the fair there!

GIRL 3: Yes, yes! The current swamiji wore green clothes that day! So, they have continued the old tradition in the ashram all these years! Our swami must have worn green robes to commemorate that historical meeting between Bande Nawaz and Shivalinga Swami. But of course, we didn't know this story when we were there.

OLD MAN: Even if he'd been a king, he couldn't have done more for humanity! After all, what can a king do? Dig a lake, make a road or plant trees on either side of the road, what else? Today, there are 360 mathas named after this boy swami in the southern country! These ashrams are places which quench people's thirst for knowledge. I had the privilege of seeing that holy matha. That boy swami was no ordinary man. He dreamt Godlike dreams! He had enough goodness in him to regenerate a whole nation! I saw the matha. His grave is there.

GIRL 2: And then?

OLD MAN: Then I came to Bidar!

Scene 2

(*The palace of the Bahamani Sultan of Bidar, King Allauddin. He is lying on a bed, groaning in pain. He also looks worried. His daughter-in-law, Begum Nargis, is nursing him. She looks dejected.*)

ALLAUDDIN: (*To the begum*) Allah struck me with this illness at this age. In a way, he bound me hand and foot, and made me bedridden. We can't trust our neighbouring kings, not even our officers—those *tarafdars* and *khilledars*. We must keep our eyes peeled for trouble at all times. Can't say who will backstab us, when and where. On top of that, Humayun has a terrible temper. Now, you, you must shoulder all the responsibility, my daughter! Me . . . now . . . in another moment, I might draw my last breath and . . .

(*Meanwhile, his son Humayun enters*)

HUMAYUN: How is our revered father's health now?

BEGUM NARGIS: It's the same.

HUMAYUN: It seems His Lordship sent word for me . . .

ALLAUDDIN: (*Getting up with difficulty*) Yes, Son! A great man has come here. He's waiting outside. Apparently, he is

121

a brilliant man famous all over Iran. They say that his intellect is unmatched in all of Iran. He was a minister. But because of some political turmoil, he left Iran and came to our country as a horse-trader. It seems he met our religious guru, Khwaja Kirmani, in Iran. And he came to our kingdom to see Khwaja Kirmani's son who lives here in Bidar. He wanted to get this holy man's blessing. Then he decided to come see us. Begum, you stay here. Son, you be here too.

HUMAYUN: Isn't it wonderful that such a big man has come here?

ALLAUDDIN: Not only wonderful, Son; our revered Kirmani, who sent word to us about Gawan from Iran, said that it was a great blessing for us! Let's see what kind of a person he is. Sit down. (*Humayun sits*) Who's there?

SERVANT: (*Enters*) Your Highness!

ALLAUDDIN: The horse trader from Iran who has come with two horses? Bring him in.

(*The servant goes out and brings Mahmoud Gawan inside. Gawan salutes the king and the others there. He sits on the chair pointed out to him*)

HUMAYUN: Sir, are you the honourable Mahmoud Gawan?

GAWAN: I am Mahmoud Gawan, sir. Khwaja Kirmani asked me to meet you. He must have sent word that I would be visiting you.

ALLAUDDIN: Yes, Khwaja Kirmani has already done that. My dear sir, this is my first son, Prince Humayun. This is his wife, Begum Nargis.

(*They exchange greetings and sit*)

ALLAUDDIN: We are extremely happy to see you! To tell you the truth, we're almost as happy as we would be if we saw Khwaja Bande Nawaz. This is the first time you are visiting our country, right?

GAWAN: Yes, huzoor! I was set to go to Delhi. But I came to Gulbarga in southern India because . . . for one thing, to see an experiment that Khwaja Bande Nawaz had conducted here. And the other purpose was to meet Khwaja Kirmani's son and get his blessing.

ALLAUDDIN: The experiment conducted by Bande Nawaz? What's that?

GAWAN: The experiment to bring harmony between the Hindus and the Muslims?

ALLAUDDIN: Khwaja Gawan, what you said is right! Ah, what a great man he was! As soon as he arrived here, he became extremely popular! People of all faiths, castes and religions readily became his devotees. In every city there rose mathas in his honour. You should attend his death anniversary which will be hosted here very soon! Our daughter-in-law goes there every year. By the way, did the revered Kirmani say anything about your staying with us?

GAWAN: He did, huzoor! I am grateful for your affection and trust. If you think I could be of service to you, I'll stay back here, my lord!

ALLAUDDIN: Really? That's a great relief! Such things happen only by Allahu's will. We wanted you here. But even before we sent word, you arrived! Isn't there some mysterious link between these events? Your great political experience, administrative skills, your valour in the war field—shouldn't our kingdom also benefit from these? Son, Humayun, arrange royal hospitality to this esteemed gentleman. You rest in the Chandnighar guest house, sir. Our son will come there and see to it that you are comfortable. Is that all right?

GAWAN: Huzoor, your great love and this hearty welcome have overwhelmed my heart! From this moment, I'm your servant. I'll do what you say.

ALLAUDDIN: Humayun, take him there.

(*Humayun invites Gawan to join him. They both leave together*)

ALLAUDDIN: Ah, this is the one good thing I did in the last days of my life. This will be of great benefit to the kingdom! See, he looks like a tall coconut palm! There is the life experience of all the Arab lands in him. By what our holy Kirmani says, this Gawan is no ordinary man, mark my words! Great war strategist. It seems he mapped all the moves in the wars his uncle fought! Can you imagine? They never lost any war in which he participated! So you can gauge his ability. If we make him our diwan, he will bring us everlasting fame! Isn't this a wonderful thing?

BEGUM: True, Your Highness! (*She turns to the door*) Oh, the doctor is here!

ALLAUDDIN: Thank God, my daughter! I have this feeling that I won't live for long . . . I have come to a state where I can't even get up from the bed! Ha, Daughter, wonder what the southerners will say to this. We must take them into our confidence. If we ask them about appointing Gawan as our diwan, they'll say, 'We're here! We can accomplish any great task you set for us . . . so, why bring in foreigners?' Then they'll try to push one of them before us. They don't like foreigners. And our Humayun is such a short-tempered young man. Anyway, you are here. Manage all this in the future!

(*He cooperates with the doctor who treats him*)

Scene 3

(Inside Chandnighar guest house. Dim lights. The dining hall. In the kitchen, two or three women are arranging the table for dinner. Humayun and Gawan sit opposite each other at the table. All leave except Neeli and another woman. Neeli is wearing a saree.)

HUMAYUN: This is Chandnighar. From now on, you will stay here. (*To the women*) The arrangements should be perfect. Everything clean and hygienic. We don't want too many people in the kitchen. Neeli, only you serve the food.

NEELI: Yes, huzoor!

HUMAYUN: We had heard of you even before you came here. The horse you gifted us is very intelligent, sir!

GAWAN: That horse is of the best Arabian breed. He will give his life for his master.

(Neeli brings the drink and a few small glasses. She sets them on the table. Humayun points to her)

HUMAYUN: This is Neeli! A Hindu girl. She will arrange your meals from tomorrow. Because of her blue eyes, we call her Neeli.

GAWAN: Neeli? Sweet name! What you've said is true. Her eyes shine like blue stars!

HUMAYUN: Our women wear sarees which cover their bodies fully. Neeli is very good-looking, isn't she? Are you married, Gawan?

GAWAN: I am married with children. I have a daughter this girl's age.

HUMAYUN: You are ahead of us in everything, fine! Do you intend to get your daughter here?

GAWAN: I haven't thought that far yet. (*Neeli is serving dinner*) I didn't even come here to stay. I wanted to trade horses. The idea was to come here first, then go to Delhi, and return to my country. Staying back with you is a new development. But as long as I am here, this Neeli, this Sapphire, will be my daughter!

SERVANT: (*Enters in a hurry*) Lord, His Highness's health has worsened suddenly. Begum has sent for you urgently!

(*When they hear this, both get up in a hurry and leave*)

Scene 4

(Tarafdar Turk's house. His well-wishers, many southern Deccani people, nobles, wealthy amirs and other administrators have gathered there.)

TURK: This is too much! Have you ever heard of something like this? The moment the king sees him and comes to know that he is a foreigner, he trusts him implicitly and gives him all the royal honours!

AMIR 1: No, sir! I have never heard or seen anything like this! What a sham and what a shame! Just unheard of.

NOBLE: How should a king be! What is his status, his stature and honour! Instead of being conscious of all this, our king goes and holds this foreigner's hand and begs him to come save us and our country. Never seen a king like this until now!

KHILLEDAR: Brother, doesn't look like we Deccanis have any luck! We keep extending our hospitality to every foreigner who walks in.

AMIR 2: Living without any self-respect is a sign of cowardice. I can't do this!

KHILLEDAR: The king doesn't trust us. Nor does he let go of us.

TURK: We must wait and see, Khilledar! We must be far-sighted. Who's he? A hero? A warrior? Just another ordinary mortal? Is he power-hungry? Woman-crazy? What's he? We still have no idea.

AMIR 3: What was he in his country? How was he? We must ascertain this from someone who knows. We can't just go by his words; otherwise he'll claim that he was the sun and the moon of his land, and since he's left there's neither been a sunrise nor a moonrise in that place!

KHILLEDAR: You're right. If our country is only to be run by foreigners, why do we leave our homes, children and wives to go to war and die for it?

AMIR 1: That's right!

TURK: You know what's more? Before he died, the sultan gave the orders to make him our diwan.

KHILLEDAR: Sure, how essential!

AMIR 2: If he is such a heroic warrior, we've to wait and see him in the war field. If he's something else, we've got to wait and watch for that too.

NOBLE: He hasn't shown himself to us as anything yet. Let him do that first. We'll do something about him then.

TURK: Even before a foreigner makes his worth known, our king goes and gives him a high place above us and presents him with all the honours. So why should he even try to prove anything at all? He'll think, 'Let those bastards imagine whatever about me, who cares!' It's only we who worry, right?

COMMANDER: If the king trusts him fully, isn't it so much less of a worry for us? Will he win us a war? Let him. Will he take care of the administration? Let him. Old tax, new tax, this tax and that . . . will he collect all those taxes? Good. From now on, we can simply shift the blame on him for all our defeats and losses. Let's not bother too much about this now. If anything else happens, we'll see. We'll cross the bridges . . .

SERVANT: (*Enters and whispers something in Turk's ear*)

TURK: It's over! It seems our king has gone to heaven. Let's go and bid him farewell.

(*Everyone is surprised. They leave with downcast faces*)

Scene 5

(*The court of the Bahamani king. Humayun and Gawan are sitting there. No one else has arrived.*)

HUMAYUN: Khwaja Gawan, now that you have become one of us, we'd like to confide in you about something.

GAWAN: Please do so, huzoor!

HUMAYUN: Ours is a kingdom full of problems. None of our neighbours have such troubles. Our army is divided; it comprises two groups—southern Deccanis and the foreigners—that is, local people and those who have come from foreign lands. In the court, those who sit on the king's right are the foreigners, and those on the left are Deccanis. They hate each other. Sometimes, they even get into street fights. We try telling them that they both are in our service and so should get along with each other. But they point to each other and say, 'Tell them that.' We kings are just mute witnesses. Their hostility continues in the war field too sometimes. They never cooperate with each other. Actually, in the wars, those who clench their teeth and fight until they win or die are the foreigners. But whenever we point this out, the Deccanis simply sneer at

131

the foreigners and lose interest in fighting altogether. We need your help in this matter. (*He suddenly remembers the meeting*) Hey, Karim, where are you?

KARIM KHAN: (*The servant enters*) Here, huzoor!

HUMAYUN: Where are they? The amirs, nobles, khilledars and tarafdars? Did you go to everybody's house and inform them about the meeting?

KARIM KHAN: I have sent messengers to every house, huzoor! They all replied that they would be here for the meeting.

HUMAYUN: What more should we do? Do we have to send the palace band to bring them here? Send someone else and tell them that the king and Khwaja Mahmoud Gawan are waiting for them. Tell them it is an urgent political matter . . .

KARIM KHAN: Yes, huzoor! (*He runs*)

HUMAYUN: It's not as if their houses are far off. 'A foreigner is here, right? Let him wait. After all, we are local people.' This is how they think and so arrive late. Just watch.

GAWAN: Or maybe there's some real problem? Anyway, they are going to be here, right? Let's wait and see.

HUMAYUN: Gawan, you still don't know the games these crooks play. They'll be here now, yes. But see how they are already thinking of ways to wriggle out of their responsibilities.

(*The amirs, tarafdars, commanders and others start arriving one after the other. They all exchange greetings*)

TURK: Huzoor, I pray that God gives you the strength to bear the loss of our sultan!

HUMAYUN: I am grateful for your good-hearted prayers, Turk! Friends and well-wishers of this kingdom, I must inform you of an unfortunate incident that happened even before His Highness, my father, passed away. The Telangana chief, Jalal Khan, has gathered a band of thugs and risen in revolt against us. Whenever something untoward happens in our family, this Jalal Khan has the habit of attacking us exactly at that time. Now, we must put an end to this. We can't sit quietly, saying that this is a period of pollution for our family since our father has died. I have called this meeting to get your urgent suggestions and advice.

TURK: Since this is a sensitive issue, we beg Your Lordship to let us know the next course of action.

HUMAYUN: You say it is a sensitive issue? Why, Turk?

TURK: Just this, my lord! As you mentioned, not only in the capital but all over the kingdom, people are in a period of pollution. What's more, the rebels are not strangers. They are relatives. In this instance, you should advise these rebels and dissuade them from going to war. I don't think they will disregard your words.

GAWAN: But these people know the circumstances we are in already, and yet they are taking advantage of it! They may be relatives, but I don't think they'll withdraw even if we talk to them.

AMIR I: Considering how sensitive the situation at home is, and then the fact that this enemy is related to us, I suggest we keep the king here and send someone else to the battlefield.

COMMANDER: What does that mean?

TURK: Just this: Gawan is a great military strategist, a brave general who has never lost a war. If he could go to the battlefield, support us in this terrible situation, and bring us victory, wouldn't that be wonderful?

GAWAN: If someone who knows the location well can come with me, I'd be happy to go.

(*Turk looks pleased*)

TURK: Not only that. Jalal Khan is a relative of the king's. If our lordship were to go with Gawan to the war too, who knows, Jalal Khan might even have a change of heart. Then there would be no war at all! Everything might turn out smoothly. If not, there was to be a war anyway. With both Gawan and His Highness being there to deal with it, even if it happens, we're sure to win.

AMIR 2: But we need someone strong to watch over the kingdom here. If Turk agrees to . . .

TURK: What! Should I send the king to the battlefield and sit here like a coward? What is the use of my loyalty to him then? But still, I'm only the king's servant and must follow his orders. Sure, it is difficult to stay back in the kingdom without him. But what does one do in this situation? It's duty!

HUMAYUN: We'll take Turk's useful advice. Gawan and I will go to Telangana. This is the decision I have taken after today's meeting. Turk, you should stay and take care of the kingdom's welfare, all right?

TURK: Your orders, huzoor! Khwaja Mahmoud Gawan is a warrior who knows no defeat. Let him go with you to Telangana. We'll watch over the kingdom, being particularly careful about what mischief the Vijayanagar and Konkan kings might want to do.

HUMAYUN: Excellent! We will return victorious, of course.

(*Everybody leaves except the king and Gawan*)

Scene 6

CHORUS/OLD MAN: In King Humayun's leadership, and with Gawan at the helm, the Bahamani army set off for Telangana. The Telangana fort is small, but because of the dense forest around, it's almost impregnable. There is a small river next to the fort. Humayun's Bahamani army had built its camps on the other bank of the river. But even as it was moving towards the camps, Jalaluddin's Telangana army attacked suddenly and almost defeated it. At this point, Gawan rode his horse into the fray and fought brilliantly. He scared the enemy horsemen. Then, even as the Telangana army was reeling under the shock, he changed his course all of a sudden. He pounced on the enemy soldiers from a different direction and ambushed them. And before they could even understand what was going on, our great military strategist, Gawan, was standing right in their midst. He had tricked them nicely. Taken by surprise, the Telangana army scuttled away in fear. Ah, the enemy had just lost the war!

Scene 7

(*The tents on the riverbank outside the city. Four men are patrolling outside the sultan's tent. Gawan enters.*)

GAWAN: Two men are getting off a boat. Do you see?

SOLDIER: Yes, huzoor.

GAWAN: If they turn towards the sultan's tent, one of you must immediately come and let me know.

SOLDIER: Yes, huzoor.

(*Gawan enters the tent. Humayun is already up. He is sitting on a chair*)

HUMAYUN: Come, come, Khwaja Gawan! I must tell you how astonished and happy I was when I saw your bravery in the battlefield yesterday! You stood in the forefront, and inspired and rejuvenated our tired army. Your war tactics simply baffled the enemy. Ah, Gawan! I hadn't seen such daring in all my life . . . astonishing!

(*Suddenly, the soldier enters*)

SOLDIER: (*To Gawan*) They have come, huzoor. They are now arranging some gifts and tributes that they have brought on a tray. They asked for permission to enter here.

GAWAN: Who are they?

SOLDIER: It seems the Telangana sultan sent them.

GAWAN: Huzoor, you must stay inside. Don't come out until I call you.

HUMAYUN: (*Surprised*) Okay. You showed us your war tactics yesterday. Let's see what new tricks you have up your sleeve today!

(*Humayun goes in through a cloth partition. Gawan sits on the sultan's chair in great style*)

GAWAN: (*To the soldier*) Send them in. All four of you should wait outside, but come in the moment I call for you. Watch out for any signals I give with my eyes, even the tiniest ones. Now go, let them in.

(*The two messengers come in with the tributes*)

BOTH: (*Bending*) Badshah, King! Peace be with you! Salutations!

GAWAN: Salutations!

MESSENGER 1: Huzoor, we are nobles at the palace of Sultan Jalal Khan. I am Asad Khan, he . . .

MESSENGER 2: Samiullah Khan.

MESSENGER 1: Our master Jalal Khan has sent us to you with these tributes and a message. Shall I read it, huzoor?

MESSENGER 2: (*Gawan gestures for them to go ahead. Messenger 2 reads the message*) Here's the anxious message Sultan Jalaluddin Khan sends in this letter:

> Badshah Humayun, Peace be with you!
> We are related by blood. The death of Badshah Allauddin, who was like a father to us, has shocked us immensely. At least now let us forget our enmity and become brothers. These words come from my soul. This is what we have decided. We are sending you this gift as a token of our friendship. If you accept this and say yes, we'll meet you today. For anything, we await your reply.
>
> Yours
> Jalal Khan

GAWAN: (*Nodding with great solemnity*) Yes. Be it so!

MESSENGER 2: Do you accept the gift, huzoor?

GAWAN: I do.

(*One messenger proffers the tray. At the same time, he tries to stab Gawan with a dagger hidden under the tray. Gawan, who had already guessed this was going to happen, holds the messenger's arm and twists it. 'Soldiers!' Gawan shouts. Instantly, the four soldiers waiting outside enter and arrest the two messengers. The commander also arrives*)

GAWAN: (*To the commander*) Find out who sent these men. You must interrogate them properly. If they answer truthfully, fine! If not, sever their heads from their torsos, then throw the torsos into the river, but keep the heads with you. We must exhibit them in Bidar.

COMMANDER: Yes, huzoor!

(*Humayun emerges slowly from inside. He too is shocked after hearing what all has happened. The soldiers bind the hands of the messengers from Telangana and take them away*)

HUMAYUN: Gawan, I just can't thank you enough! If I'd been there instead of you . . . can't say what would have happened! How did you know they were dangerous, Gawan?

SERVANT: (*Enters*) Huzoor, your trusted man, Karim Khan, from Bidar . . .

HUMAYUN: Let him in. (*To Karim Khan, who rushes in*) Arre, Karim Khan! What news do you have?

KARIM KHAN: (*He is agitated*) Huzoor, a great tragedy has happened! They spread false news that you died in the Telangana war. Then all those traitors said the throne shouldn't be empty. They crowned your brother Sikandar Shah, then took him in a procession all over the city, Your Lordship . . . (*He collapses*)

HUMAYUN: (*Gets up and bellows*) Is that true, Karimya?! Your mother's—if you are telling lies, I'll . . .

KARIM KHAN: No, Appa! I witnessed it all. I came running here . . . Your security officer, the kotwal, sent me to call you back, Appa . . .

GAWAN: Looks like the news is true, Your Highness!

HUMAYUN: Ayyo, Ayyo! Which son of a bitch plotted all this? How did my brother Sikandar Shah agree to it? Is he also a party to this . . .

KARIM KHAN: Turk actually led the procession. You please come and see for yourself. Come and see what's happening there, Appa!

HUMAYUN: Treason! Betrayal! But even if some bastard hatched this conspiracy, how did my brother Sikandar Shah agree to it? Whoreson!

(*He gnashes his teeth in anger, his mouth is foaming with blood. Gawan steps in front of him*)

GAWAN: This has really happened, my king! You must leave for your kingdom immediately. Take five hundred loyal soldiers with you. Looks like this war was just a veil—a fake war orchestrated to conceal something else. I'll find out what it's all about. If necessary, I'll win it and come back. But huzoor, I think you should go back to the kingdom right now.

HUMAYUN: Did you see, Gawan . . . the games siblings play? He might even have taken Jalaluddin's help. I think they knowingly set Jalaluddin on us and sent us here. There, they crowned my brother . . . Who? Who're they? Didn't my wife know of this?

(*He tears his clothes in anger*)

KARIM KHAN: But she took your permission and went to Bande Nawaz's death anniversary, don't you remember?

HUMAYUN: Yes . . . yes. This wouldn't have happened if she'd been there. That Turk must have engineered all this. He was always seething with jealousy inside. So, the moment my father died, he must have thought that we all were ignorant little lads and he could gobble this kingdom up!

GAWAN: Your Highness, there is no doubt that some gruesome conspiracy has taken place in the kingdom. Please don't lose your temper or your wisdom. Go back to the capital calmly. I will finish this Telangana war and follow you to Bidar soon. God be with you, leave now!

HUMAYUN: So be it, Gawan! You come back victorious. Karim, come, let's go . . .

(*He leaves with Karim Khan*)

Scene 8

(*Enter a messenger with a drum and four soldiers following him. The messenger stands on a raised platform.*)

MESSENGER: Hear, hear, all our subjects of Bidar! His Highness, Sultan Humayun, has not died in the great Telangana war. Yet, his brother Sikandar Shah was crowned king here, right? But not only has King Humayun not died in the war, he is returning to the city with his army after winning a great victory against the enemy. He is coming back to the accompaniment of the military band.

Therefore, all the subjects are hereby informed that Sikandar Shah's ascension to the throne yesterday was unlawful and stands annulled. We inform you that Sultan Humayun continues as the emperor of the Bahamani kingdom.

None of our subjects should create any disturbance in the capital. They should not form groups and talk in the streets. As wise and peace-loving citizens, you must all stay in your houses. This is Sultan Humayun's order. Soldiers are patrolling the streets now. They will punish and fine those who violate the king's order . . .

(*The messenger and his followers exit in a disciplined manner*)

Scene 9

(*Four men stand talking in the street.*)

CITIZEN 1: How many kings does a kingdom have? One or two?

CITIZEN 2: Two! One real king, and another fake!

CITIZEN 3: Okay, of the two, who is real and who's fake?

CITIZEN 2: The one who sits on the throne is the real king, and the one on a chessboard? He's fake!

CITIZEN 1: But he who sits on the throne is crying, the one on the chessboard is laughing!

CITIZEN 2: Wait, wait, they'll switch places soon. Let's see what happens then. Look, do you hear the drums and trumpets?

CITIZEN 3: But why are we hearing these sounds so long after the king returned?

CITIZEN 2: One is deaf, the other blind. The blind one didn't see the other come, the deaf one didn't hear the other talk.

CITIZEN 4: Ayyo, ayyo, what's happened to this kingdom?

CITIZEN 1: Shut up, please! Just think: we'll have to pay taxes to both kings!

Scene 10

(*On a street in front of a big house. Four or five people emerge. They slowly come out one after the other and stand there.*)

CITIZEN 1: What, sir? King Humayun has always been a bit crazy. He returned and started a big hue and cry.

CITIZEN 2: Apparently, Humayun's men butchered all those who took part in his brother Sikandar Shah's crowning ceremony; they might have killed thousands already!

ELDER CITIZEN 1: Seems eight or nine corpses have fallen in the palace!

ELDER CITIZEN 2: They thought Turk did this, so they sent the army to his village to catch him. By what I hear, when they couldn't find him there, they burnt the whole village.

CITIZEN 1: That maniac Humayun! Rogue! Can't say what he'll do or won't!

(*A soldier who has escaped comes and joins the group*)

SOLDIER 1: I've heard there are numerous corpses of both men and women in the palace!

(*Another soldier runs on the stage beating his chest*)

ELDER CITIZEN 1: (*Stopping him*) Hey, hey, are you crazy! Come here. What's the news? Why are you beating your chest like that, you fool?

(*He pulls the soldier and tries to console him. But the soldier continues to scream 'Ayyo, ayyo' and beat his chest. Somebody gets a pot of water from the palace and splashes it on the soldier's face. The soldier wipes his face slowly*)

ELDER CITIZEN 1: Hey, madman, why are you beating your chest like someone crazy? What happened to you?

SOLDIER 2: They killed Sikandar Shah, cut him to pieces and fed the pieces to the tigers in the cages! He actually cut his blood brother into pieces and threw his . . .

(*Yet another soldier runs on the stage screaming, 'Ayyo! Ayyo!'*)

SOLDIER 3: Come, come, hey . . . somebody has killed King Humayun! Not a fly is alive in the palace. Men, women, corpses and corpses! That rogue Humayun is lying dead on his bed . . . he's bled so much . . .

ELDER CITIZEN 2: What? What did you say? Is the king dead too?

SOLDIER 3: Yes, yes, Grandpa! I saw it with my own eyes, Grandpa! You go see it . . . you go see . . .

(*Some people run towards the palace. Others don't want to be bothered with this business. The same cry, 'They killed the king! They killed him!', is heard from every corner of the city*)

ELDER CITIZEN 2: How did the sultan die, sir? Who could have killed the king?

SOLDIER 3: Nothing human did it . . . a she-devil was hiding in there. The king went and drew that devil to his bed. When he was about to pounce on her, the devil wrestled with him, threw him over, and ran away! But there was another devil, a male one, standing there with a dagger. He stabbed the sultan repeatedly and escaped. Sir! Yappa! God knows where that devil disappeared! The devil leered, sir! But before you knew . . . vanished! Disappeared into the dark!

PART II

Scene 1

OLD MAN: (*Imagining himself to be Gawan*) I won the Telangana war. That was easy. I didn't even get off my horse; I directly went to the capital, and from there straight to the palace! But the palace was a graveyard. In the large courtroom, there lay corpses. I spotted someone—a body almost on the verge of death; it had survived, holding on to a straw of hope, and sat hugging the leg of the throne. Begum Nargis! She was sitting there, eyes wide open. But she didn't see me. Obviously, she was lost in thought. I left without disturbing her.

(*Old man is back to himself now. He is narrating the story again*) Begum Nargis continued to sit there lost in thought. She was in great despair. That dream palace of luxury, a home filled with rainbows of joy, had now collapsed at one unwise stroke! No neighbours to help. All around were enemy kings, waiting to gobble the kingdom up. The only people you could think of as your people were the Deccanis. But they were the ones who had conspired first.

The only support left was Khwaja Mahmoud Gawan! The one who ought to be used with tact was Turk!

After thinking about the two for a long time, the queen summoned them to the palace.

Scene 2

(*Large courtroom. The begum sits at the foot of the throne, resting against it. Leaning against her shoulder sits Ahmed Shah. Gawan and Turk enter. They both bow to the begum and take a seat. The begum is wearing a burqa.*)

BEGUM: Honourable Gawan, the king came to Telangana, didn't he?

GAWAN: Yes, Mother! The morning hadn't broken yet when we got the news that Sikandar Shah had been crowned here. The moment Humayun heard this, he became livid. He gave me the responsibility of fighting the war, and rushed to the capital. I win the war and come here. This is the scene I see!

BEGUM: Turk, you were right here, weren't you?

TURK: In all my life, I hadn't seen the king in such a rage, Mother! Before I could even ask him why he was so angry, it seems he had given orders for the village—the same village he had gifted me once—to be burnt to ashes. I felt that I couldn't pacify him, so I ran away to my village. But my village was burning. So, I rushed back here in the morning. And I saw this scene! There, my village had turned into ashes. Here, His Lordship lay like this . . .! You tell me, Mother . . .

GAWAN: There are many important tasks waiting for us, Mother! This is not the time to sit musing on causes and effects. With enemies all around, we can't afford to waste any time. Our subjects are waiting anxiously. All the responsibility is on your shoulders, Mother. Take heart and guide us now.

BEGUM: Khwaja Gawan, respected Turk, I can call you the well-wishers of this kingdom, call you our relatives, elders or even the surviving members of this family—whatever; I have only you two left now. The sultan is gone. His brother is gone too. Now, the only people left in the family, who are concerned about this kingdom, are my youngest son and you two. Everything depends on you. I am trusting my youngest son, Ahmed Shah, to your care. You may save him, or you may not. Go, Son, touch their feet and salute them.

(*Ahmed Shah does as he is told. Both bless him*)

TURK: Who killed the king? Do you know anything about that, Your Ladyship?

BEGUM: In that gory exhibition of the sultan's anger, who knows who was inside the palace, and who was outside? Who deserved punishment? Who gave that punishment? Who are the victims? Who are our people? Who are the outsiders? Nothing makes sense, no rhyme or reason to anything that happened that day. When I came back from Bande Nawaz's anniversary, I saw scores of corpses in the palace. Don't even ask me about how many fell outside the city! What's the point in remembering things which will only make us more afraid? The matter of punishing those responsible—let's not bother about that now. What we want right now is to make sure that this royal and ancient Bahamani household doesn't fall apart. Therefore, we must crown Ahmed Shah and establish some order.

GAWAN: You're right, Mother—what we need now is exactly this. If you are not too particular about waiting for an auspicious moment, let's go ahead and crown him today.

TURK: But don't we need to make some preparations for anything at all?

GAWAN: Of course, yes. But not now. A kingdom without a king looks tempting to our already hungry neighbours. They may even claim that they want to save our kingdom in order to take it. I think there are also people in here who might want to strike! Before we begin to feel such greed for power, let's have a king, at least a nominal head of this kingdom. Everything will fall into place later.

TURK: Did anyone tell you about those greedy insiders, Gawan? Have you actually seen them or what?

GAWAN: I might have said what I did, but I can't actually point out such people to you. I can only caution you about the dangerous situation we are in.

BEGUM: Isn't it good to be on our guard?

TURK: Yes, you're right.

BEGUM: Then we will make these arrangements for now. Let's first have the coronation of King Ahmed Shah. Since he is very young, let's set up an administrative body to assist him. Khwaja Turk can take care of the ministerial *vaziri* duties, while Khwaja Mahmoud Gawan can take care of the law and order of the state. We would be very happy if Khwaja Mahmoud Gawan also took up the responsibility of the prince's education.

GAWAN: Yes, Mother. It will be my pleasure to do so.

BEGUM: This arrangement will be in place from today—from this very moment! I want this set-up to start functioning immediately.

GAWAN: As you order; I'll start this work right away, respected Begum. (*Summoning the servant*) Who's there?

SERVANT: (*Enters*) What is your command, sir?

GAWAN: Send word for the commander, minister, tarafdars, khilledars, nobles and other officials to come to the court this evening.

SERVANT: (*Bows*) Yes, sir.

GAWAN: There's another thing we need to do right now, Mother. As of now, there are four divisions in the kingdom, and each tarafdar has the opportunity of acting independently like a king. They spend all the taxes they collect. They appoint and pay their own khilledar and soldiers. This means that any tarafdar can revolt against the king anytime he wants.

Here is the immediate change I propose: let the kingdom be divided into eight parts instead of four. Then the tarafdars can't unite. In addition, let the centre control the pay of all the officials in these eight parts. If you agree, I too will become the tarafdar of one of these parts. Most importantly, you should become the president of the administrative board. This is all I want to say, Mother.

BEGUM: Brother, this will be in effect from today.

GAWAN: Then could we say that today's administrative body made these decisions?

BEGUM: Say what the decisions are, sir.

GAWAN: At the auspicious moment of the moonrise tonight, Bahamani Sultan Ahmed Shah will ascend the throne. It will take place in the august presence of the state officials, elders, nobles and others. The president of the administrative body, Begum Nargis, has given orders to this effect . . .

TURK: Don't you think this is an overhasty decision?

BEGUM: If you, who is one of the pillars of this state, express such doubts what do we do?

GAWAN: Please remember this, friends! A kingdom with traitors in it will go bankrupt. A kingdom where there is unity will always stand. I will promise this to the president of the administrative board of the Bahamani kingdom— Mother, I will never betray this kingdom which has given me food and shelter. I will keep my promise and maintain the same loyalty towards you and this land until I die.

BEGUM: What do you say, Turk?

TURK: I say the same, respected Begum. Unity is our strength. I will swear on Allah that I'll never be a traitor.

Scene 3

OLD MAN: With Ahmed Shah as the student and Gawan as his teacher, this madrasa started. The boy was surprisingly bright. That which others learn in a year, he learnt in just a month. What others could learn in a month, in a week, and what they would learn in a week, in a day. He was growing up, both physically and mentally, at an amazing speed. Soon, he grew up to be a king with an adult's mind. One day, at the end of the durbar, he asked his guru this . . .

AHMED SHAH: Father, although our kingdom is vast, we don't have enough money. We are forced to build our army with the horses left over from our neighbour, the Vijayanagar kingdom. They get lots and lots of taxes from the coastal region. We have nothing. It would have been so good if we too had the control of the coastal region, wouldn't it?

GAWAN: I'll ask you a question too. If you can answer that correctly . . .

AHMED SHAH: Please ask . . .

GAWAN: As you know, we have two groups in our army—the Deccanis and the foreigners. In the royal durbar, those who sit on your right are the foreign brigade and those on the left are the Deccanis. Do our neighbouring kings too have such divisions in their army?

AHMED SHAH: You are right, Appaji! Only we have such divisions in our kingdom. There is nothing like that with any of our neighbours.

GAWAN: Then will our king tell us why? What are the consequences of this? And what does it cost the kingdom to have such divisions?

TURK: What our honourable Gawan has said is true. We have both Deccanis and foreigners. We don't even drink the same water. But we can't change all this in a day or two merely via royal orders. Perhaps, the rift can be bridged gradually as we begin to understand each other better. However, what is the connection between this problem and what His Lordship said about merging the coastal region with our kingdom? I don't understand!

NIZAMULMULK: Our king's dream is grand, like a story straight out of a folk tale! But any expert in this matter will tell us how impossible it is for us to surpass the Vijayanagar kingdom. We shouldn't flatter the king by endorsing his colourful dreams. We shouldn't nourish his false illusions. No responsible guru would do something that dangerous.

TURK: Our king is so young. It is only natural for him to dream such dreams at this age. But don't forget that he is our only ray of hope. After all, how old is he? What is his knowledge of the world? We must think of all this, and make our young king acquire some wisdom, get a sense of reality, and not lead him astray.

GAWAN: I didn't say this to lead him astray! And it isn't so easy to gain control over the coastal region either. We need a lot of preparation. First of all, we must assess our total strength, make an estimate of what more we need, and let the king know. If you have an idea, you tell him please.

TURK: We need at least fifty thousand men. We must be able to pay them. They won't fight for some philosophy.

AHMED SHAH: Now, our nobles, tarafdars, khilledars and amirs should give of their wealth! If each one of them gives us fifteen thousand pieces of gold, that will suffice. Those who own ten thousand acres of land could gift the king gold or silver. What do you say, Turk?

TURK: I want to thank you, huzoor, for giving me an opportunity to say something first.

AHMED SHAH: This Bahamani rulership has always treated a senior and experienced person like you with great honour. Could I ask why you seem to doubt this now?

TURK: I mean, I thank you for letting me talk before Khwaja Gawan who is new to the kingdom, younger to me in years, and is also a foreigner.

AHMED SHAH: Gawan was given this administrative position because our religious guru recommended him. Moreover, all this has been done with a full awareness of his splendid record. We should not speak lightly of his stature.

TURK: Please forgive me, huzoor! It was not my intention to offend anybody.

AHMED SHAH: All right, now come to the matter at hand. Think of this matter from whichever angle you want, I just want a big army—a big army—and that army will want a salary.

TURK: It is only proper to think of the honour of the royal household. Because in the past, the royal household has never felt any want.

AHMED SHAH: That was because the kingdom never had any overarching ambition of this kind. So we had no need to ask for money from our nobles and officials. You know now, don't you? We have not four, but eight tarafdars. Till now, you used to collect all the taxes and enjoy the returns. All I ask for is a small portion of that money. Give if you want. If not, tell me you don't want the tarafdar's position. We don't want to engage in a pointless debate.

TURK: Let's think of this then: should we levy a special tax on the Hindus to procure the money you require? This is important. A kingdom cannot exist without war. War is necessary to protect the kingdom and the people. We may be a small kingdom. But we too have our ego. Really! There's no kingdom without self-prestige. At least to sustain this prestige, we'll have to go to war. And if we want war, we must also be prepared to sacrifice something for it.

GAWAN: This isn't proper advice, sir! All the subjects enjoy the fruits of winning a war equally. So, levying extra tax on only one section of the population is discrimination.

AHMED SHAH: What our revered Gawan says is perfectly right!

(*Meanwhile, a cow moos outside*)

TURK: Arre! Some animal is making a lot of noise! Did you hear it? What animal is that? Did you hear it, huzoor? Gawan, did you hear it?

AHMED SHAH: Yes, I heard it. It must be a cow, right? Appaji, did you hear it?

GAWAN: Yes, my lord. It's a cow. A household animal.

TURK: Our Gawan is a great scholar. He even knows the language of animals. Honourable Gawan must have understood what the cow said, right?

GAWAN: I certainly did! What the cow asked me was this— why're you there? Where you are, there are only wild and dangerous beasts. You should just come here and be with me instead.

(*Everybody laughs loudly. They begin to leave, still laughing. Gawan gets up*)

GAWAN: Huzoor, give me an army of exactly fifty thousand men. A month for preparation, and another for the battle. If, on the first day of the third month, the coastal region doesn't become a part of our kingdom . . .

BEGUM: (*Who is standing behind the curtain and listening, comes out suddenly*) Please, Brother, stop this! No promises and vows. Now, my lord, let us know what you think.

AHMED SHAH: We will make all the arrangements in accordance with our revered Appaji's instructions. Let all the tarafdars begin collecting the army and money from today. I believe that we are laying the foundation for our kingdom's brilliant future. Mother, give us your blessings.

BEGUM: Let it be so, Son!

(*Except the mother, son and Gawan, everybody leaves muttering to themselves*)

Scene 4

(*Turk and Nizam are alone in Nizam's house.*)

TURK: What kind of a historical curiosity is this, man! A moment's discussion decides a great kingdom's fate! Can you believe it?

NIZAM: Whether you believe it or not, this boy sultan ascended the throne sometime back, didn't he? What is the point of you and I making problems for ourselves now?

TURK: That foreigner pushed us into it in such an unholy haste. Do you think he suspects that we have an eye on the kingdom?

NIZAM: If he does, it's only natural. A day hadn't passed since Sultan Humayun went to war with Telangana, and we were in a hurry to crown Sikandar Shah. Wasn't that a stupid blunder? No wonder he got suspicious. We're lucky they still haven't called for an investigation of Sultan Humayun's death. Be happy about that!

TURK: Whatever weapon we use, it hits the wrong person. This foreigner always escapes harm. What do we do? I'm languishing here after losing everything—my house, my property, my village . . .!

NIZAM: Take heart, my friend! Your palace that used to evoke envy in every heart simply burnt to ashes! The very thought scares me . . . I shiver when I think of it. Allah!

TURK: We must bear all this, man! This experience is like walking around with fire wrapped in our clothes. That rogue Humayun, and his bloody anger!

NIZAM: But we too were hasty. That's why all this happened, okay? We thought everything was going on well. But that good-for-nothing Karimya ran to Humayun in Telangana and informed him about what was going on here.

TURK: That rogue kept uttering my name repeatedly! None of your names came out of the great Humayun's mouth.

NIZAM: This is why I say that you still haven't learnt your lesson. Don't shout like that, man! These walls have ears. Listen, in any case, that foreign fellow is bringing disaster upon himself. We'll wait patiently. That girl, Neeli? You have that wonderful weapon in your hand, right? Hide it carefully. He's already dreaming of winning a great war and pleasing both mother and son. Let him try his hand at it. It is no little matter making an enemy of the Vijayanagar empire. You shut up and just watch!

Scene 5

OLD MAN: Although the other tarafdars dawdled on collecting money and men, Khwaja Gawan started the very next day. His journey began with twenty horsemen. He set off for the Khelana region in Maharashtra.

(*There, a Marathi official, the much respected Damaji Panta, is waiting with his retinue for Gawan. The moment Gawan arrives, he honours him with a huge garland, holds his hand, and leads him inside. To the accompaniment of auspicious musical instruments like tabor, drums and trumpets, they walk in the city*)

GAWAN: Sir, you have arranged a grand welcome indeed! Look at these dancing artistes and the instruments they are playing . . .! Aha, Panta! But why have those tabor and drum artistes fastened a broom to their backs?

PANTA: This is the custom in our parts, sir.

GAWAN: Strange! I can understand their holding the instruments in their hands, but why the brooms on their backs?

PANTA: Oh, that? They are people of the Mahar caste. That is, they are untouchables, Dalits. When they walk in the city, they must clean the footprints they leave on the ground. The brooms are for that. You know, in this place, we care a lot about purity and pollution, sir.

When the Mahars aren't called forth to play these instruments, they work in the fields or other people's houses and earn some money.

GAWAN: Do they fasten brooms to their backs even when they work in the fields?

PANTA: No, only when they walk in the city. They must do that. They also hold a pot in their hands.

GAWAN: Ah, look! There are people standing at a distance and watching the procession. They have such pots in their hands. Are you speaking of them?

PANTA: Yes, sir.

GAWAN: Why those pots?

PANTA: Because these people are addicted to chewing betel leaves and areca nuts. They have to spit out the leaves they have chewed, right? But they can't spit on the ground and pollute it. So, they spit into their pots and empty them outside the city. We should keep the city clean, shouldn't we?

GAWAN: Do they have any government jobs?

PANTA: Many, sir! They collect taxes. They hand over the taxes they have collected to the government with great integrity. These people are very honest in their dealings with the government, and they are absolutely duty conscious. No doubt about that.

GAWAN: Are they more honest than high-caste people?

PANTA: Usually, they both are sincere in performing their duties, sir. See, that's the guest house. We have made arrangements for your meal there. Please come.

(*The instrumentalists stand outside the guest house. Gawan and his army go in*)

PANTA: Let all your cavalrymen wash their feet and sit for the meal. The food is ready.

GAWAN: Won't the instrumentalists sit with us too?

PANTA: They sat for their meal already.

GAWAN: Where?

PANTA: Come out, see there . . .

GAWAN: No, Panta! They are sitting away from us, outside! Why? They brought us here, shouldn't they also sit with us for the meal? How can they sit away from us like this?

PANTA: Sir, they are Mahar people, Dalits. Our custom doesn't allow them to sit with high-caste people for a meal.

GAWAN: What kind of custom is this, Panta? They celebrated our arrival with such excitement and joy. They played music and danced for us. Now, if they sit away from us, how can I not feel bad about it?

PANTA: Sir, this is a custom which has been passed down to us for many generations, from ancient times. We can't mix with the outcastes socially or eat with them.

GAWAN: Panta, don't feel bad about this then. I will go out of the guest house and sit with those Mahars to eat. Will you say yes to that at least?

PANTA: Is that unavoidable?

GAWAN: Please give me permission!

(*He gets up. Some people are standing outside, waiting for food. They are listening to the conversation between Panta and Gawan*)

GAWAN: Hey, my cavalrymen, you come too! We'll sit outside with the instrumentalists and eat.

(*The cavalrymen and Gawan sit with the Dalits for their meal. Panta is shocked.*)

GAWAN: Panta, you come and sit with us too . . .

(*He holds Panta's hand with cheerful familiarity and urges him to join them.*)

PANTA: Is that possible? No, no. You all sit, please. My people and I will serve you, come, sir. It's indeed my great fortune that I got this unusual opportunity to serve you food. I must have done something good in my past life.

(*He insists on serving them. He takes the dish from the man who has come to serve them and starts serving the food himself. Meanwhile, the Dalits approach Gawan who has come to eat with them. Some fold their hands and some bow down reverently. Gawan too exchanges greetings and sits for his meal. After the meal, Gawan gets up first. He goes to the seats placed on a platform at a distance and sits on one of them. He calls Panta, who has been serving food, and makes him sit on the seat opposite his*)

GAWAN: The meal was good, Panta. We were all terribly hungry after walking in the sun. In fact, the tasty food has composed my tummy and pacified my entire system! Like you say—'*Annadata Sukhi Bhava*'. Let the one who gives food be blessed! That's a nice saying. May Allah keep you happy, Panta!

PANTA: Ah, you only ate this bland vegetarian food. Are you really happy with it? We're fortunate to have you here, respected Gawan.

GAWAN: Okay, I have to say a couple of words to you. The Bahamani kingdom is now divided into eight parts instead of four. Of them, for one part, the part you are in, I'm the tarafdar.

PANTA: Then we're fortunate beings!

GAWAN: I'm not familiar with this land. You should help me select a popular khilledar. Will you?

PANTA: Of course, sir! I'll obey you fully and joyfully. I'll choose the right khilledar for you in a day or two.

GAWAN: This is what you call true friendship, my friend! Now, you have to accept two other requests of mine.

PANTA: Don't say request, sir! Say 'order'!

GAWAN: The Bahamani king, Ahmed Shah, is planning to go into a big war. You must help us with two things. This war isn't a minor affair. Big war. We need a lot of money. Need a big army. We need your generous help in securing both.

PANTA: (*Folds his hands, salutes and gets up*) But how can I give all this? Where will I get the money from? Revered Gawan, you walked all over the region before you came here. Did you see even an inch of green anywhere? In this wretched place, we've had no rains. There's a raging famine. I'm poor. How can I help you with money? You tell me, sir.

(*He comes and sits on the floor in front of Gawan, still folding his hands. He doesn't get up even when Gawan tries to raise him*)

PANTA: There's another scene I want you to see. Will you step this way, please?

GAWAN: (*Gets up*) Okay, let's see that.

PANTA: Look, there, those who stand holding plates in their hands?

GAWAN: Yes, who're they?

PANTA: The hungry, sir! Farmers who are desperate because there're no rains, no crops, nothing to eat. They are standing there hoping that on account of the big people who have come to this place, they will be able to get some food today. What can I tell them? What would you say to them?

(*Gawan sees them and slumps on the platform there*)

GAWAN: What's this, Panta? When there are such people in your land, how could you give me that extravagant meal? And we ate it! Don't you think this is a crime? Why didn't you show them to me earlier?

PANTA: They were afraid you might refuse your meal if you saw them earlier. So, they have come after your meal.

GAWAN: Ayyo, God! Is there anything I can do for them? Please let me know.

PANTA: If you are willing to do it, there's a way to help, sir.

GAWAN: Tell me, what can I do?

PANTA: There's a lot of grain in the government granary, sir. If you can tell the king and . . . at least this year, people will live. They will always remember you for this!

GAWAN: Fine. Do so. I'll tell the sultan. He is very generous. You distribute all the grain in his name.

PANTA: (*Joyfully*) Gawan! Gawan! Revered Gawan! What golden words you have said! You are Bande Nawaz incarnate for us. Sir, I salute you. Tell me, how many men do you need for the army?

GAWAN: How many people can you give?

PANTA: Ten thousand? Twenty thousand? I can give you hungry young men.

GAWAN: Ten thousand will do. Get ten thousand men ready and also appoint a khilledar . . .

PANTA: I'll send them to you in two weeks.

GAWAN: Wonderful!

PANTA: How do we pay for the grain in the granary?

GAWAN: Next year, if it rains and if people can pay for it. If not, we'll think of it later. But if God doesn't help you even a little, he really must be stone! We have finished this conversation. May I take leave of you, Panta?

PANTA: Gawan, you have shown Godlike mercy to us. Please look after us from time to time, sir. The moment it rains, on the day of the Guru Purnima in the Ashada month, we'll send a Mahar with the money.

(*They both embrace and bid farewell. The Dalits and the poor, who have been standing there all through, play their musical instruments and cry with joy: 'Victory to Khwaja Mahmoud Gawan!'*)

Scene 6

OLD MAN: Despite some shortcomings in their preparations, the Bahamani army set off for Belagavi on the day decided earlier. Khwaja Gawan had invited twenty technical experts from Iran to make gunpowder.

Another good thing that Gawan did was to make the Bahamani king double the soldiers' pay before they set off on their journey. This created a wonderful dynamism in the army. Soldiers forgot their tarafdars and forged solidarity with Gawan.

The war in Belagavi started as wars usually do. But later, in the mid-morning, Gawan's army started shooting at the fortress. With this lightning attack, the fortress wall caved in. The Vijayanagar army surrendered. Gawan appointed a trusted person as administrator there. His army set off for Goa next.

Even Goa fell as easily and unexpectedly. The whole coastal region came under Bahamani control. That was the day Gawan had set as the deadline for the victory for himself—the first day of the third month! The victorious army drank and danced all night. The next morning, the messenger made an announcement with his drum . . .

MESSENGER: All the subjects of the Bahamani kingdom, hear! Our army has achieved a wonderful victory over the Vijayanagar kings. We feel proud to announce that Belagavi, Goa city, and the coast are all a part of our Bahamani kingdom now. The sultan has ordered that we should celebrate this historic victory through the month. For all these festivities, arrangements have been made to grant funds to every village and city in the kingdom . . .

Scene 7

(*Capital. In front of Gawan's house in Bidar. Sultan Ahmed Shah, his mother, Begum Nargis, Turk, Nizam and the tarafdars enter. Gawan's doorman makes way for them to enter the house, but they tell him, 'Please go and ask revered Gawan if we have permission to enter.'*)

SERVANT: (*Comes into the house*) Huzoor, His Highness and his mother have come to meet you. They are asking if they can come in.

GAWAN: Fool, why didn't you let them in?

SERVANT: They told me to go in and check with you.

GAWAN: Come, come.

(*Gawan comes out in haste, bows to the king and his mother, and brings them in. He points to a seat and stands waiting*)

KING: Revered Appaji, how can I describe the immense joy of this victory that you've given us? I never thought that I would enjoy such a great moment in my life! I can hardly speak, I am so overwhelmed with joy!

GAWAN: What, my lord . . . if you say such things . . . I feel greatly embarrassed! All this belongs to you, my lord.

BEGUM: No, Brother! You've brought joy and fulfilment to the entire Bahamani family. We are grateful to you.

TURK: You won the war precisely on the day you had set as your deadline! Then you promptly gifted the coastal region to the sultan. Khwaja Gawan, can there be a greater achievement than this?

NIZAM: For the first time in the history of Hindustan you used gunpowder and achieved success. Khwaja Gawan, we just can't adequately express our gratitude to you . . .

AHMED SHAH: As a token of all our gratitude, in my revered mother's presence, with these tarafdars as my witnesses, I am requesting you to be the diwan of our kingdom now. This had been my esteemed grandfather Sultan Allauddin Khan's wish before he passed away. I am happy to be fulfilling it at least now. Here, I am giving you my royal gown as a gift. I'm also presenting you with the highest award of our kingdom, 'Jahan'. I request you to accept these and swap your gown with me.

(*For a moment, Gawan is overwhelmed by joy. He doesn't know what to do, looks confused. Then, shaking with nervousness, he slowly exchanges his gown with the king's. He salutes the begum, the king and everyone else. All applaud and express their joy.*)

AHMED SHAH: Revered Khwaja Jahan Gawan, from today, you are the diwan of our kingdom!

This is the diwan's royal seal. Please keep it safe. Don't ever lose it. If you were to lose it and someone makes use of it, you'll be held responsible for it, all right?

BEGUM: That is, if this seal is stamped on any letter, we assume that you have approved of it. Nothing is legal without this seal.

GAWAN: I understand. But do I deserve this honour, Mother? I begin to have some self-doubt now.

BEGUM: Brother, you must accept this, please!

(*Gawan receives the royal seal, presses it reverently to his eyes, and salutes the begum and king*)

NIZAM: Gawan, what the sultan has said is completely true. Huzoor, I second your words and your decision to make Khwaja Gawan the diwan. Khwaja Gawan is a good person. He is unparalleled in his speech, manner and scholarship. Whether he stamps the royal seal or not, his word is law to us. I congratulate the new diwan of the kingdom!

GAWAN: Allah, let me never doubt you or your power! May your voice seep through my words and manner. Let goodness and wisdom always be alive in me. I accept this position in your name.

(*He folds his hands and bows to all*)

(*Turk and Nizam move aside and whisper to each other*)

NIZAM: It's your turn to act. Don't forget that he is the diwan of the Bahamani empire now. But you have that divine blue weapon. Neeli? Don't forget it!

Scene 8

OLD MAN: Done, right? Gawan's story has reached a certain point. He became the diwan of the kingdom . . . then . . .

GIRL: In the following years, he got wells dug, lakes filled with water, built roads, planted trees on either side of those roads . . .

OLD MAN: Aha! But after Humayun's assassination, Turk was still alive, wasn't he? Neeli, who had run away to her village, fearing that she'd be charged with the sultan's murder, continued to stay there. Gawan, like everyone else, thought that Neeli had been one amongst the many corpses that had fallen in the palace on that day of chaos and mayhem, that day when Humayun had been murdered. So, he never looked for her.

But . . .

Turk hadn't forgotten how his village had been set on fire and his mansion burnt. He went to Neeli's village, searching for her, and told her, 'Nobody except me knows that you are hiding here in your village. Remember? You were the last person I saw with King Humayun before he died in the palace that day. The suspicion of murdering him has fallen on you now. But if you want to be saved once and for all from this, you must do what I tell you: You see, we must send a letter stating that you are innocent. And it should reach Sultan Ahmed Shah without Gawan's knowledge. So, your only hope of being saved depends on stealing the paper with the diwan's stamp on it. Go there, go quickly . . .' He urged her. Neeli cleverly got into Gawan's house when he wasn't there. She stole a paper of that kind, gave it to Turk, and was happy thinking that her problem had been solved.

Nizam and Turk, who had received that stamped paper from Neeli, wrote a letter to the king of Odisha. They wrote that letter as if it was from Gawan. Then they promptly gave it to the sultan, pretending that they had accidentally intercepted Gawan's trusted messenger and found it.

A week before the sultan was to order the court to assemble, they spread poisonous rumours about Gawan's treason all over the city.

GIRL 3: Did the sultan believe all this?

OLD MAN: (*Too engrossed in telling the story*) People gathered in groups and began to talk, to discuss the matter of Gawan's letter.

As usual, even in this instance, there were two groups. If the Deccanis formed one group, the foreigners formed another. The Deccanis knew that this was Nizam's trick. But they wanted Gawan to be sent back to Iran, and for Nizam to occupy Gawan's position in the Bahamani kingdom. The foreigners, however, trusted the sultan's mother.

That mother knew who Gawan was and who was Nizam. She had gauged them, and knew their worth. She was aware who had worked for the kingdom and how much. This letter must be a creation of Nizam and Turk's, she felt.

Gawan also got to know this news. He realized that it was a fake letter. He set his spies and guards to investigate the origins of this letter and find out who was behind it.

BOY 2: Didn't the sultan know how much Gawan had done to serve his kingdom?

OLD MAN: Even if he knew . . . you see, rumours and tales that evil people carry have a more powerful impact.

GIRL 1: But wasn't the begum right there? Wasn't she the president of the administrative board?

BOY 3: And didn't that Neeli know the news?

OLD MAN: The news reached her too. She was utterly shocked. The moment it became clear to her that she had put the life of the man who had cared for her like a daughter in danger, she came to Turk's house with her husband.

Scene 9

(*Turk's house. Nizam and Turk sit opposite each other. They are drinking.*)

TURK: People are going mad with anger. They are barking insults at the diwan behind his back, calling him a traitor—someone who betrayed those who fed and sheltered him . . . these are the names they are calling the diwan.

NIZAM: Until now, none of our machinations had worked so well, right? He is struggling to get to the root of this mystery.

TURK: The sultan has sent for him. But this son . . . he keeps putting off meeting him. He keeps warding the king off by saying that he will be there, that he will be there soon, and so on. Meanwhile, the sultan keeps sending for him.

NIZAM: Yes, but what does the begum say?

TURK: It seems she was telling her son what a wonderful man Gawan was and declaring that whatever he did was beyond criticism. She even prophesied that all the talebearers who had carried these stories about Gawan to the king would one day wring their hands and stand looking at Gawan in frustration.

NIZAM: But the king is stubborn. He is easily swayed by tales.

TURK: That is our one and only hope. You know why? We can't trust the military. We don't have the kind of power Gawan has over it.

(*Suddenly, they hear a knock on the door*)

TURK: Who's it?

NEELI: Me, Neeli, huzoor.

TURK: Neeli who?

NEELI: Didn't you recognize me?

TURK: Who are you, Neeli?

(*He opens the door, she walks in*)

NEELI: Ayya, have you already forgotten my name? You came to my village looking for me. I listened to you and brought a sheet of paper from Gawan's house, remember? That Neeli . . .

(*He pulls her inside suddenly and shuts the door*)

NEELI: You still haven't recognized me? Okay, I'll leave then.

TURK: (*He does not want her to leave*) Wait, wait, I remember you now. Come, sit. Hey, who's there? Get some water for this young lady. Relax. Tell me slowly . . . why have you come here?

NEELI: Looks like you still aren't sure who I am!

TURK: I know. You were a servant, a cook in Gawan's house. Your name is Neeli, right?

NEELI: And?

TURK: And what?

NEELI: I got the paper with the royal seal on it from Gawan's house and gave it to you.

TURK: Yes, I wrote about you in that letter. Poor thing, Neeli is an innocent girl. She didn't murder the king . . . this is what we wrote.

NEELI: You showed that to the sultan. Therefore, he is planning to get Gawan to his court and kill him, right? Do you think I am still so dumb that I believe all your lies? I have realized what you and Turk were up to when you wrote on that paper with Gawan's seal.

TURK: Ayyoo, poor man! We don't know a thing. Did Gawan tell you all this?

NEELI: Why do you need Gawan to tell you all this, Appa? Even cowherds are talking about it. I heard that. Do you realize who I am?

TURK: Che, you are a very clever girl! Tell me, tell me now . . . why have you come here? Who sent you here? Look, Neeli. You must know one thing. I am a powerful tarafdar in the king's court. I can do anything I wish. Kill or save you. Be careful!

NEELI: I knew that you were a big man. (*With irony in her voice*) But didn't know that you were such a big man, really!

TURK: Now you know, right? Shut up and listen to me. I gave you a bit of importance because you were a maid in Gawan's house. Because I thought you were one in a thousand. Someone who told the truth. Someone frank.

NEELI: Yes, very truthful and frank. Shall I tell you what I see? You are a mad dog. A dog who bites anyone he comes across and enjoys that.

TURK: Abababa! A maidservant in a foreigner's house has the gumption to call Tarafdar Khwaja Turk a mad dog! Now, I know you fully, you see?

NEELI: Now, you know, don't you? Tell me, will you give that paper back to me, or shall I go and inform the begum?

TURK: Neeli, Mother Neeli! Who are you? Who am I? Who is Khwaja Gawan? Aren't we all people who have eaten the salt of this palace? You are still a young girl. You should wear nice colourful sarees. Wear gold. Enjoy all this in life . . .

NEELI: My husband will take care of all that. Now, will you give me that letter, or should I go tell the sultan everything that happened?

TURK: Oh, has it come to this? Okay, wait, I'll get the letter . . .

(*He pretends he is going into the house, then turns back suddenly and tries to strangle Neeli. Neeli, who has guessed this move already, grabs his hand, and using a wrestling tactic, fells him to the ground. She strangles him. Turk dies of this unexpected attack.*)

NEELI: Ayyoo, rascal! You died even before I could catch you on what you did! Now, where're you, Nizam, hey!

(*She looks inside the house. Nizam, who is watching all this, gets scared. He escapes from the back door. Neeli's husband enters, holds her hand, and leads her away*)

Scene 10

(Tarafdar Nizamulmulk's house. A few other tarafdars, amirs and nobles who are close to him have gathered there.)

NOBLE: But what has happened now is shocking, sir! It hasn't even been two years since Khwaja Gawan became the diwan, and our Turk gets murdered . . . what does it mean? Is this the failure of governance, or of the diwan? Did you see the corpse's face? How troubled it looked? Like there was a curse on him or something . . . che!

AMIR 1: You mean it was all because of Gawan?

NOBLE: But why? What is the connection between Turk and Khwaja Gawan?

AMIR 1: There must be someone who knows the background to this murder. Is Turk an ordinary man? He is the tarafdar of a part of the kingdom. If he has been murdered, and the diwan doesn't even know of it, isn't it rather strange? Is there no law and order in this kingdom? Can anybody kill anyone? Is there nobody in charge of things? Can you believe it? A tarafdar being murdered right in the capital?

AMIR 2: Whether you believe it or not, the murder has been done, right? How did it happen? Why? This is the secret knot you can't undo.

TARAFDAR 1: As it is, Turk hated the sight of Gawan. The more he got jealous, the more Gawan shone!

AMIR 1: Turk didn't even like the begum. He'd often talk disgustingly about her.

AMIR 2: He only loved himself. He spoke badly of everyone else. Especially about Gawan—the moment he heard the name, he'd get blue in the face.

TARAFDAR 2: He must have died after getting blue in the face!

AMIR 3: You know, they strangled him!

AMIR 2: This is the work of a strong man. This murder wasn't done by just anybody.

AMIR 3: Why did that Humayun Sultan order Turk's house to be burnt?

AMIR 1: That's an old story. Let's not get into all that now. Just think of our current situation. We need great patience now to deal with things. King Ahmed Shah is so unstable. He isn't the same today as he was yesterday. We can't even trust our army like we could earlier. Already, the foreigner's poison has infected their blood. God knows what cunning he showed in the battle . . .

AMIR 2: People are scared. They don't know what will happen in the kingdom.

TARAFDAR 2: God knows what else awaits us until the court assembles tomorrow.

AMIR 3: When the court assembles tomorrow, we must bring up the matters of the madrasa and Khelana.

NIZAM: Yes, yes. We must bring them up. Such matters shouldn't be suppressed.

AMIR 1: I think you all are hiding something!

NOBLE: What are we hiding, man? What do we have to hide, sir?

TARAFDAR 1: Amir, you are referring to Turk's dagger, right?

AMIR 2: Che, che, not that, sir! It seems that was found in Humayun's tummy. What I am asking about is . . . they are saying that a wall of difference has risen between the sultan and diwan of late? I want to know why.

NOBLE: Only this tarafdar, our Nizam, can tell you something about it, Appa! That's because this tarafdar is the one who has close and daily interactions with the king. But if everybody keeps their mouths shut, how can we know?

AMIR 1: Perhaps Nizam doesn't tell us because he thinks that we are cheap people who count their loose change!

NIZAM: Okay, okay, listen—it seems that the diwan wrote a letter to the king of Odisha. He was sending it with his secretary. But that man got intercepted. God knows what was inside that letter! Why did the sultan's men catch that secretary? I have no idea!

Apparently, the sultan has kept the letter with himself. He has sent word for the diwan repeatedly for the past two days. But the diwan keeps evading him, telling the king that he's coming . . .

Whatever! This is all I know. The story doesn't seem to have a head or a tail!

AMIR 1: Anyway, the court will assemble. The diwan must open his mouth there.

NIZAM: I believe he will. But I don't know anything about the wall of difference coming in between the sultan and diwan.

AMIR 2: Okay, but Turk and you were great friends, weren't you? You should know something about what happened with Turk, at least?

NOBLE: Oh, we completely forgot that we must go to the court! It's time. Come, let's go.

(*They disperse*)

Scene 11

(*Khwaja Jahan Mahmoud Gawan's house. He is looking at the door.*)

GAWAN: Who's there?

SERVANT: (*Enters*) Huzoor.

GAWAN: Hasn't the security officer, the kotwal, come yet?

SERVANT: No, huzoor.

(*There is a noise outside. Suddenly, Gawan notices a human foot peeking out from under the closet and realizes that someone is hiding inside*)

GAWAN: (*Stabs at the foot with his sword*) If you come out, you're saved. Otherwise, you will die in there!

(*A woman emerges from the closet*)

GAWAN: Another step, and your story is finished! Cross your arms, put them over your head, and turn around.

(*The woman does as he commands*)

Oh, you? Neeli? Sapphire? My daughter! You stupid girl, I had been searching for you! Chi, idiot! There was news that Turk had you killed. How come you are alive?

NEELI: I didn't know that the revered Gawan would recognize me so quickly!

GAWAN: How can I forget someone whom I called a daughter? Tell me, where were you? After Humayun's murder, you disappeared. I am seeing you only today. Why have you come now? To murder me or what?

NEELI: I have already murdered you. Sealed your fate!

GAWAN: You mean you killed Turk?

NEELI: Yes! But everybody thinks that you did it.

GAWAN: Oh, God! How did Turk come into your story? When? Why?

NEELI: He was planning to tarnish your reputation in front of the king. So, I finished him.

GAWAN: Now, there are not one, but many questions you must answer. First question—what is the relationship between you and Turk?

NEELI: That day, when Sultan Humayun returned from Telangana, he got everyone killed. It didn't matter if they were relatives or friends. He even burnt Turk's village. That night, my friend Gulabi and I were hiding in the palace kitchen. It was a dark night. I heard the king shout outside, 'Hey, Neeli! Bring me some liquor.' I went with the liquor cask and placed it in front of him. When I was about to turn around and leave, he tugged at my saree. I fell on his dirty mattress. But I got up instantly, threw him over, and ran away. As I tried to get out, I saw someone standing in the corner. It was Turk! He stood there holding a dagger. He whispered, 'Run away to your village. If you don't, they'll know that you killed the king and will kill you,' he warned. So, I ran away to the village with my husband.

GAWAN: Ha! But how did you have the strength to throw the sultan over?

NEELI: This is something you don't know, Father! I've learnt wrestling. I never knew my father or mother, but I had an uncle. He taught me wrestling in my childhood. My husband is also a wrestler. A national champion! You know how I met my husband? How we got married? You see, I had heard a lot about this wrestler.

One day I taunted this man, fought with him, and felled him to the ground. People who had gathered there lifted me up and cheered, 'Ho, ho! Neeli won!'

GAWAN: Oh, now I know that you have another side to you! You grew up like a boy? But how did the marriage happen?

NEELI: The champ who fell to the ground got up. Ashamed, he buried his face in his hands and ran off to his house. He sat in there with the door shut. I followed him, sat on his doorstep and declared, 'I will marry this man only!' Later, my uncle got us married. He died soon after that. You are the first person to call me daughter.

GAWAN: Sure, I called you that. My daughter is also boyish like you, though not as much. Do you wrestle with your husband even now?

NEELI: Oho! Whenever I do, I win.

GAWAN: Okay, now tell me, why did you kill Turk?

NEELI: I had been living quietly in my village for a while. After you became the diwan, he came straight to my village. He brought up the issue of the king's murder, threatening me, 'You will only be saved if you go and bring a letter with the royal seal from the diwan's house. If not, everyone will know that you killed the king. And Gawan himself will hang you for it.' My husband too thought that we should listen to Turk. I came to your house, stole a letter with the royal seal on it, and delivered it to Turk's house. 'Good, good!' he remarked. Nizamulmulk was there too. Seeing the letter, they said something I couldn't understand and laughed. At that moment, I realized that I had done something wrong. You know everything he did after that, don't you? Anyway, yesterday, I went to his house and demanded the letter back. I threatened him saying that otherwise I'd tell the sultan everything they had done.

He closed the door and tried to strangle me. I said, 'Why do you take the trouble, sir?' and strangled him!

GAWAN: You better get this out of your mind right away—first, that I am your father. It is because of this that you've not been able to. Instead, know that I am the diwan of the Bahamani kingdom first . . .

NEELI: Today, I am wearing the saree you gifted me. That means I'm your daughter. You may be ashamed of being my father. But be that at least for today. Later, if you don't like it, you can stop. But this much is true: Turk killed the innocent dumb girl in me. Now, the sultan has summoned you regarding that matter with the Odisha king . . . you know, I've been killing you repeatedly. It started with the letter Turk and Nizamulmulk wrote in your name to the Odisha king! Then, I went and murdered Turk. People think you did it. Now, the task before me is to inform the king of what really happened, I mean about the letter that those two wrote to the Odisha king.

GAWAN: What's the use of that? The sultan may not even believe you.

NEELI: If he doesn't believe me, it's his fault. If he thinks that only what the big people say is true and what the ordinary people say is false, what does the king's law mean?

Shall I tell you the truth, Father? The first time you called me your daughter, I went mad with joy. But when I murdered you by bringing the letter with the royal seal to Turk, I was disgusted with myself. I'd wronged you and bruised my soul. I can see my soul bleeding and oozing pus. (*Crying*) Appa, I'm looking at the Sapphire whom you named. Her voice has nothing to hide now. There is no quiet inside her, like that which her father has. I'm a woman of flesh. Not a man who exists in the intellectual realm like my father. I must go to the king and confess the truth.

GAWAN: You wring my heart, my child! No, Daughter! They have poisoned the king's mind with their lies. I don't want him to harm or humiliate you. I want you to live, my daughter.

NEELI: You have taught me that we should never be afraid of telling the truth. So, should I stay back home, feeling afraid? The king has already sent for you. You shouldn't go. If you go, I'll go with you too.

SERVANT: (*Enters*) The elder citizens and some of your friends from Gujarat have come. They want to meet you urgently.

STRANGERS: (*Five or six men rush in at once*) Huzoor, we have come from Gujarat to make sure that you are not in any danger. We were sent by our king, who is a friend and a well-wisher of yours.

COMMANDER 1: Sir, both the southern and the foreign soldiers have come together. We want to protect you. Please don't say no. Give us an opportunity to serve you.

COMMANDER 2: Yes, we are all ready. None of us is with the treacherous tarafdars. We're with you. We won't let anything unjust happen to you. You shouldn't go. Come away with us for at least a couple of days. Let's go to the tomb of Bande Nawaz.

(*Elder citizens enter*)

ELDER 1: Sir, unknown and mysterious fears haunt our minds. Please don't give us some philosophical argument and let us down.

ELDER 2: Sir, we know the dangers of power. If power and position have come easily, there's a lot more danger there. Very soon, the man loses not only his eyes and ears, but his ability to reason. Because of this king's stinking sins, deadly diseases have surfaced and are spreading all over the streets, Gawan!

GAWAN: The king has consciously invited this kind of danger. What can I do? I have no way of stopping this.

ELDER 2: Why not? Make a tentative deal with the king. Doesn't that solve the problem? Give some pretext and postpone your visit to the court by a day. The king will soon realize the truth.

ELDER 1: Say, he doesn't accept this pretext. You can write another letter saying, 'Yes, I did write that letter to the king of Odisha. That's true, please forgive me,' and send it to him. We will be playing for time, at least for a day.

GAWAN: It is a crime to confess to something you haven't done. If I am struggling so much because of something I haven't done, imagine what might be waiting for me if I give a false pretext! No, I can't agree to this.

ELDERS: Ayyoo, we're going to see horrible sights! Maybe the gory scene of our eyes and ears being plucked and eaten away by those men—those beasts. God, God!

GAWAN: Friends, there cannot be a breach in my loyalty to the king. A minister who is loyal to his king will gain merit both on earth and in heaven.

NEELI: (*Crying*) Listen to them, Appa. Are these people your enemies? If you stay away from the king for a day or two, he'll figure out the truth himself. He'll realize that what he got was a fake letter and change his mind. Only a day or two, Appa . . .

COMMANDER 1: Huzoor, we have three thousand horses. We'll take you to Gujarat. We're willing to give our lives for you. Please go with us, sir!

GAWAN: Friends, my beard turned grey in the service of our king's father. If it turns red with blood in the son's service, let it! I am not scared. Please don't press me about leaving now.

NEELI: Appa (*crying, she holds onto Gawan's feet firmly and sits there*), Appa, don't go, please . . .

GAWAN: I served the king all these years honourably, my daughter. Never committed any crime. I have faith that the king will act justly. I don't think he'll listen to lies and punish me. But if God decides that this should happen and gives him an evil mind, I must suffer. Let go of my feet, daughter.

NEELI: Then I'll go with you too . . .

COMMANDER 1: Please come away with us, huzoor . . .

GAWAN: If I escape, it is like disobeying the king's order. It would be revolt, ingratitude. No, friends. Daughter, I have never lied in my life. I have served the king with honesty. If he has the good heart to understand this, let him. There's a God above, Daughter. The king has sent word for me, so I'll go. If you wish to go with me, do so. If not, don't. Shall I leave now, my friends, my daughter?

(*He exits.*)

Scene 12

(*King Ahmed Shah sits in the palace porch, drinking. He has the letter which Nizamulmulk gave him in his hand. The latter too sits close by. Begum Nargis enters and stands at the door.*)

BEGUM: Son, Sultan! Will you come in for a minute?

AHMED SHAH: Why, Mother?

BEGUM: There's something I want to talk about privately with you. Come, Son.

AHMED SHAH: (*Tries to get up, sways and falls back on his seat. He settles down there*) Can't you say whatever you want to right here?

(*Begum Nargis looks at Nizam with dislike. He gets up and walks outside. The begum takes off the burqa and comes in*)

BEGUM: Is it true that you sent soldiers to arrest Khwaja Jahan Gawan and bring him here?

AHMED SHAH: Yes. So what? I have sent many people already. He doesn't come. The king is sending people to fetch him since morning. What does it mean if he still hasn't turned up? The diwan doesn't obey the sultan. So, why should anyone care?

BEGUM: You have been drinking since you got up, Appa . . . would you even understand what I am going to say?

AHMED SHAH: If I have to wait for the diwan for hours, what else should I do while I wait? Go ahead, tell me whatever you want to say.

BEGUM: Didn't your soldier say that Khwaja Gawan is on his way?

AHMED SHAH: I am waiting, right? Are you done with what you wanted to say, Mother?

BEGUM: Just one other thing. When your father Humayun made a mess of things and died, you were only a small boy. Then Gawan came, put you on the throne, educated you, made you king and protected you. Remember that!

Your huge ambition was to win the coastal region. He won it for you from Vijayanagar. You honoured him then, remember? He not only mentored you in politics and administration, he shaped your thoughts. He taught you practically everything about life, didn't he? He is someone who always protected your interests first and thought of his interests only later. Remember also how two north Indian kings invited him to their court when he was already diwan here. He refused.

Who're the people who are telling tales? How have they really helped you? Think of all this. Understand their motives behind telling these tales.

Look, see, he has come. Get up and greet him.

(*Gawan and Neeli enter with two soldiers. Soldiers withdraw slowly. Neeli salutes the queen and stands behind her. Nizam enters*)

GAWAN: My salutations to the honourable Sultan!

AHMED SHAH: (*Still sitting*) Please sit.

(*He indicates a seat. But Gawan doesn't sit*)

GAWAN: I have come as an accused, I shouldn't sit, my lord!

BEGUM: (*Folds her hand and salutes Gawan*) Who are you? And who is he? What does it mean to call yourself an accused before your disciple? Someone who wishes you ill has given this letter. The sultan is just a little upset from reading it. This is something which happens wherever there are talebearers. This isn't new to you, is it? Why are you still standing? Please sit.

AHMED SHAH: Mother, if you can be quiet, I want to say a couple of words to Gawan.

BEGUM: All right, Son. You talk between yourselves.

(*She withdraws. Neeli also withdraws*)

AHMED SHAH: Diwan, let me ask you some questions. One, how many students are there in the madrasa you are running? How much money is spent on them? How much of it is from royal funds? What about the expenses of building the place? Have you maintained the accounts? If so, where are they?

GAWAN: I run the madrasa with the money I get from trading horses and my salary as diwan. The madrasa has nothing do with the sultan. Anyway, all the accounts are with a man called Hasan Gilani. You send for him, he'll give you the details.

AHMED SHAH: All right. This work has already started from yesterday. Another charge:

> You couldn't collect the taxes from Maharashtra.
> On top of that, you went ahead and distributed
> all the grain in the royal granary to those people
> to gain cheap popularity. Who is responsible for
> the losses incurred?

GAWAN: My lord, those people were in a wretched condition because of the drought. It wasn't possible for any human being to collect taxes from those people groaning with hunger.

NIZAM: But this situation didn't arise last year when we collected taxes. There was drought even then.

GAWAN: There has been drought for the past two years, huzoor. Last year, there was the crop from the year before. Therefore, they were able to muster something out of what was left from the year before and pay. It got difficult this time because the drought continued. Those who gave ten or twenty last year folded their hands and begged, 'This year, you give us something.' Farmers and the poor cried, beating their stomachs that if we didn't give them something they'd die of starvation.

NIZAM: You describe it all so vividly, Gawan. You prove that you are a fine poet. Those people too found a nice way to cheat you. They started beating on their naked tummies, and whoever saw them felt great pity, right?

GAWAN: I said all this to the sultan out of compassion for the poor, sir. Not to show off my poetic talent. Nizam, if the poor and the farmers are starving, it becomes the sultan's duty to take care of them.

NIZAM: Are you saying that the sultan doesn't know this?

GAWAN: I'm just reminding him.

AHMED SHAH: What should we do now, Gawan?

GAWAN: I heard there are good rains this year. They'll give.

AHMED SHAH: If they don't?

GAWAN: Tell me what fine I should pay, I will do that.

BEGUM: (*The moment she comes to the door, Nizam steps back*) Does the sultan know what he is saying? Are you in your right senses? Is this the way to question the diwan of the kingdom? It rained this year. They will pay. That's it. Those who must collect later are you and your lackeys.

AHMED SHAH: Mother, you shouldn't have interfered.

BEGUM: Now, I should ask you directly. I have seen how revered Gawan has served this kingdom. As the queen mother, I will always remember the man who put her son on the throne. I am the president of the administrative body. Don't I have the right to intervene?

GAWAN: I beg of you, please be quiet, Mother.

AHMED SHAH: Now, finally, just answer me this. This is a private letter. Written by the diwan. Let everyone hear. Come here, Nizamulmulk.

(*When Nizam comes closer, the sultan gives him the letter and asks him to read it aloud. Nizam reads*)

NIZAM: The letter written to the Odra king by Diwan Mahmoud Gawan:

> I cannot describe the atrocities committed by the Bahamani emperor who is given to excessive drinking. I have had enough of all this. It is very easy to win the Deccan. There are no good officials in the Rajamahendri region. You can attack this region from your side. Many officials and army men are on my side. I will come and join you with a large army. Both of us can defeat the king and take over the land. Then we can split it between us later.
>
> Yours truly.

AHMED SHAH: Show the letter to Gawan.

(*Nizam shows the letter. Neeli comes up front*)

GAWAN: (*Sees the letter*) The seal is mine, but the writing is not. I am not the one who got this written either. This is fake. Allah, who guides my speech and manner, the God who gives me wisdom and lights up my life, I will say that with Allah as my witness, I didn't write this letter.

AHMED SHAH: Then whose royal seal is this?

GAWAN: The seal is mine, the letter isn't.

NEELI: Now, I'll tell you something. Huzoor, you must listen to me . . . Mother, Amma . . .

BEGUM: What, Neeli?

NEELI: I stole this paper with the diwan's seal from his house and gave it to Turk. Turk handed this letter to Nizam even

as I watched. This Nizam wrote the matter in it, whatever
it is that you see now. Then both of them looked at it and
laughed. At the time, I didn't know what they were actually
writing. But I have been witness to their manipulating the
letter. I swear on Allah. This is true.

NIZAM: Wonderful! Doesn't this woman know that Turk is
dead? Who is this woman? If the peasants and servants
start giving witness, will there be any law and order in
this land? If royal justice has fallen to this level . . . this is
ridiculous, huzoor . . . It won't surprise me if this woman
says she killed Turk.

NEELI: Yes, I killed Turk.

NIZAM: (*Laughing*) Did you hear this, huzoor!

NEELI: Ayyo, ayyo!

AHMED SHAH: Who is this woman?

BEGUM: Sultan, she is from the palace. Our servant. Although
she is Hindu, we kept her in our service because she cooks
well. King Humayun had appointed her to serve Gawan.
Please listen to what she has to say. She never lies.

NEELI: I went to Turk's house with my husband two days ago.
It was night. I knocked on the door. He shouted from
inside and asked who I was. I told him my name was
Neeli, the same Neeli who gave him the stolen letter from
Gawan's house. He came out immediately and asked me
to step in. My husband stayed outside. When I went in,
he asked me why I was there. He warned me about trying
to be too smart. He wanted to know who had sent me
there. Then I demanded the letter I got from Gawan's
house. He cooled down a bit. He went on in an insulting

manner, saying that he had taken pity on me because I was some wretched servant in Gawan's house. But now that I was trying to put my price up, he'd give me what I deserve . . . He shut the door suddenly, lunged at me, and held my neck. I shrugged his hand off easily and strangled him instead! That fellow was finished! This Nizam, who hid inside, didn't come out at all! He stood inside shocked and open-mouthed. This is what happened, sir!

NIZAM: Is this possible, huzoor? Discussions of matters like these shouldn't slip into mutual recriminations. This is not befitting the dignity of the court. Huzoor, although you are young, you are aware of our subjects' anxieties. If you permit me, I'll say a couple of words.

AHMED SHAH: Go ahead.

NIZAM: Jahan Gawan's choice of words, style of speaking, and the smile he flashes . . . we were all charmed by these. So, we immediately accepted everything he said and became his followers, right? None of us have his magical powers, huzoor. But my problem is this—is this a kingdom of Hindu rulers? Or is it an Islamic empire? I am beginning to doubt it now, huzoor! Gawan appointed a Hindu woman as his cook at home. He used her as a spy to get to know the palace secrets. He controls the palace affairs through this strategy. Does anyone among us have this great art of hoodwinking? We have a world famous university here. But we don't know of it! Our diwan sends letters to Hindu kings to attack our kingdom. What's all this? If this woman has killed Humayun too, the palace doesn't even know of it!

BEGUM: It was a dagger with Turk's name on it that was found in my husband's stomach. You know who killed him, don't you?

AHMED SHAH: It is wrong of you to interfere. This is a sensitive legal matter. None of us is an enemy of Gawan's. But should we remain quiet even when he has done something treacherous like this?

BEGUM: Ayyo, Ayyo . . . what's wrong with you? He has protected you like a father . . .

AHMED SHAH: Why do you keep saying that he is like my father again and again? Turk used to make snide remarks about this when he was alive. Tell me, what is the relationship between you and Gawan? Why do you tell me repeatedly that he's like my father? Tell me . . . tell me . . .

(*Both the begum and Gawan are shocked. Gawan holds his head in pain, the begum is about to collapse. Neeli steadies her. The court becomes still*)

BEGUM: This family is finished, revered sir!

SERVANT: (*Enters*) My lord, a Mahar from Khelana has come. He insists on seeing you this moment.

AHMED SHAH: Send him in.

(*Even before the king says this, the Mahar enters. He looks this way and that. But he doesn't look at the king*)

MAHAR: Aha, you're here? I recognized you, revered Gawan. Sir, I have brought the taxes from our region in Maharashtra. Not only has Panta paid the taxes for this year, he has also sent the price of the grain you gave us from the royal granary. Take this.

(*He puts a heavy bag down and opens it. Everyone is astonished to see the huge amount of gold coins in it. While they are staring at it in alarm, the Mahar goes to Gawan*)

Revered sir, please count all this. We've paid up everything.
Write a letter saying that all the money we owe you has
been paid up. And give me my wages, sir!

GAWAN: Like Allah, you came in and saved me during this
difficult hour. What is your name?

MAHAR: Mahar Vitthala.

GAWAN: Aha! Mahar Vitthala! What a divine name you have,
man! I'll tell you the truth, my friend—you are really
Vitthala! Please convey my regards and thanks to the
honourable Panta. Don't forget it!

(*He folds his hands and salutes Mahar Vitthala. Gawan
picks up a coin from the bag the Mahar has deposited on
the floor and gives it to him. He holds Vitthala's hand and
stands there looking at him. He is ecstatic with happiness*)

MAHAR VITTHALA: I'll certainly convey that. Can I leave now?

GAWAN: You gave us so much joy by your mere presence, Appa!
May you have a pleasant journey back.

(*Mahar Vitthala salutes again and leaves. Gawan is still
folding his hands. Suddenly, Panta rushes in like a mad
man*)

PANTA: Revered Gawan! (*He comes and grabs Gawan's hands*)
Gawan, please forgive me, forgive me, sir! I couldn't pay
the taxes at the promised time. I am telling you the truth.
We have the same difficulty this year too. The same
drought continues, Appa! You listened to our troubles like
a God then. I am telling you the same thing this year too.
Please forgive me, Gawan—I am not lying. If you want,
come to our city, see the state of the land and the water,

and decide for yourself. Show your mercy just this year, Appa . . .

GAWAN: Panta . . . Panta (*shaking the crying Panta*) What has happened to you? See, there? Do you see the bag full of gold coins? Your Mahar Vitthala came here, said you had sent this to us and left it here! Didn't you send Mahar Vitthala?

PANTA: (*Looking at everybody's face*) Really! (*Alarmed*) Did Mahar Vitthala come here really?

GAWAN: Mahar Vitthala came, told us that Panta had sent last year's tax arrears, plus the price of grain from the royal granary—and gave all this.

PANTA: (*Runs to the begum and folds his hands*) Is what he says true, Mother?

BEGUM: Yes. He gave it and left just a moment ago. He also mentioned your name.

PANTA: Is that true, Sister?

NEELI: Yes, I saw him give it.

PANTA: My God! I didn't give any money to anyone, revered Gawan . . . I don't even have a tamarind seed to give to anyone, sir! So much money! Wait . . . what did he say his name was?

GAWAN: Mahar Vitthala!

PANTA: Oh, oh! Had Mahar Vitthala come? (*He collapses on the ground*) Did you come as Mahar Vitthala and appear in front of Khwaja Gawan, my God? Did you keep the promise of Guru Purnima and save me, my father? My father Vitthala, Vitthala!

GAWAN: (*In tears*) You didn't send him. Since there were no rains, you were not in a position to send him at all. Despite this, Lord Vitthala came in the form of this Mahar and paid up last year's arrears and the price of grain from the royal granary! See, he has poured all the gold here! Why would Vitthala come here but to save me and shower his mercy on me! I am blessed, indeed blessed, Panta!

PANTA: Lord Vitthala himself, pleased with your devotion, came here and poured gold to pay the tax debts, didn't he? Gawan, Gawan, sir, you (*He folds his hands and then embraces Gawan, weeping*) What a great saint you are! . . . Touching you has washed away my sins, I am blessed indeed! (*He cries. The begum and Neeli fold their hands and stand watching all this. The bhajan 'Jaal Mahara Pandarinatha' is heard in the background*)

AMIR: Huzoor, please conclude these proceedings soon. Looks like the army is getting restless. People are gathering around the palace.

AHMED SHAH: Who's this fellow? Who let him in? Throw him out . . . Gawan, one last time, isn't the royal seal in the letter yours?

GAWAN: Yes.

AHMED SHAH: Then you tell me this. What is the punishment for treason?

GAWAN: Execution.

AHMED SHAH: (*To the executioners*) Take the life of this person.

(*Immediately, two executioners come and stand on either side of Gawan*)

BEGUM: (*Comes out instantly. Facing the sky, she kneels*) Ayyo, God! Look at this wretched sultan who is murdering his own good name! You give him some wisdom, my God!

AHMED SHAH: Hey, you two, didn't you hear what I said?

GAWAN: Huzoor, can I please say my last words?

AHMED SHAH: Make it quick!

GAWAN: Huzoor, you have already become the disciple of some devil. You cannot understand my words now. All my joys of serving the kingdom have turned to ashes at this last moment of my life. You didn't see the history hidden behind you. That is your misfortune. I don't have to be grateful to you!

Mother, Begum, you protected me like a mother. My heartfelt thanks to you! Neeli, Sapphire, you became my daughter, wrung my heart and taught me that when politics turns foul, it is our duty to protest. My blessings to you!

I thought that God, who was a friend of Bande Nawaz, hadn't extended his friendly hand to help me. But . . .

Allah! Are you listening to me? Like Shivalinga and Bande Nawaz, I too served the people, with a little difference. In times like these, everything is topsy-turvy! Nature revolts. Even seasons race helter-skelter like scared cattle. Cause and effect have lost connection. Therefore, now man's fate must be decided only by ruthless politics. The main inspiration behind the rise of the Bahamani dynasty was the blending of the two religions. It was born with the promise of bringing politics and dharma, the ethics, together. But now politics doesn't need morality.

But dharma is actually rooted in morality, right? So, I talked of the need for wisdom in politics. I wanted to resist the divisive forces of caste, religion, sect and all political differences. I tried to unite the land and the people. But the sultan didn't understand anything. When I felt sad that all that I did after coming to this place was futile, Allah came in the form of Mahar Vitthala! He broke my pride, stood like a naked shining light, and gave me immense confidence again. He made me feel that what I had done wasn't futile after all. Now, I will face my fate calmly. But efforts like mine should continue. Do you hear me, my God?

(*A thunderous noise. We hear a voice from the sky*)

I heard you, Gawan! There will indeed be a blend of wisdom and politics someday. You must wait until then. I must live in the *abhang* song, and you must become history's eye. We must wait. We must wait, Brother. Let's wait for that great day to come!

Din hari hara[1]
Din hari hara

(*Gawan signals to the executioners to strike and bends his head*)

NEELI: (*In a high voice*) Stop this! I cannot see the murder of Gawan, the Father of Truth.

AHMED SHAH: Hasn't she gone yet?

NEELI: I'll go, wait, sir! I hoped that at least you would realize the truth of revered Gawan. But there is no sense of gratitude in you, is there? Even when God Himself came and shook hands with Gawan, you didn't see that. I knew then that people like you are incapable of realizing such things.

NIZAM: What impudence in front of the king!

NEELI: Yes, wasn't it only after I gave you the letter with Gawan's seal that you wrote all those lies on that paper?

NIZAM: My lord, this is a bit much!

AHMED SHAH: Seize her by her hair! Throw her out, Son!

(*A soldier comes towards her to push her out. She kicks him as if he is some animal. He falls facedown on the ground. Everybody is shocked. They stand gaping at this sight. Neeli goes to Gawan as if nothing has happened, touches his feet and salutes him*)

NEELI: Wait, already dark smoky clouds are floating over the palace! The rain of fire is imminent!
   Father, bless me. Bless me so that I may be born your daughter in my next birth.

GAWAN: Yes, my daughter! (*He presses his hand on her head and blesses her*)

(*Neeli is about to leave. As she is leaving, the sultan signs to the executioners to kill Gawan. They swing their swords and Gawan collapses*)

'Ayyo, murder! Murder! Gawan's murder!' (*Neeli screams and falls on the ground.*)

BEGUM: *Inna lillahi wa inna ilyahi raajiwoon*[2]

(*Far away, a song is heard. People rush in singing the bhajan*)

Jhala mahara pandarinatha . . .
Kaay devachi sango batha . . .[3]

NOTES

The Bringer of Rain: Rishyashringa

1. Traditional folk play popular in Karnataka. The myth revolves around Lord Krishna and his jealous wife Satyabhama who wants him to get the divine parijatha (sometimes called night-flowering jasmine or coral jasmine) from Lord Indra's garden.
2. Loose end of a saree, or *pallu*, as it is called in Hindi.
3. Humorous and mostly nonsensical verse used while playing a game.
4. The pot borne by the mourners has the 'guggul' wood burning in it. Symbolic of death.
5. Leaves that symbolize victory. Like a laurel.
6. Bhandara is a mix of turmeric powder which is offered to, or smeared on, the idol. It is seen as holy. Given to devotees as a form of blessing.
7. A rural ritual which is supposed to bring rain. A boy walks on the streets bearing a glob of cowdung on a platter on his head. He goes to every house in the village. People pour a little water on the glob of dung and give the boy some grain as charity. The boy dances with the platter on his head and leaves.
8. Sharanas are saints who belong to the Veerashaiva religion. The word also refers simply to the devotees of Shiva in this religion.

9. 'Maama' is like 'Mava' or 'Maava'. It refers to a lover or a prospective husband.
10. The special festival days celebrated in honour of Goddess Ellamma of Savadatti in north Karnataka. Men cross-dress as women (*jogti*s or temple dancers) and dance on those days.

Mahmoud Gawan

1. *Din* in Arabic means religion. The lines suggest the bringing together of Islam and Hinduism. In addition, they incorporate both the devotees of Shiva and Vishnu (Hari and Hara) into this vision of communal harmony.
2. 'Surely, we belong to Allah and we must return to Allah.'
3. Lines of a well-known Marathi abhang: 'God Pandarinatha became a Mahar; What can we say (or know) about God's ways!' The line challenges caste divisions.